The Drama of the Mother-Child Bond

*What Every
Woman Should Know
About Motherhood,
Career and Children*

Ada Anbar, Ph.D.

Robin Publications, Phoenix

ISBN: 0615640443
ISBN 13: 9780615640440
Library of Congress Control Number: 2012908404
Robin Publications, Phoenix AZ

ALSO BY DR. ADA ANBAR

How to Choose a Nursery School
The Secret of Natural Readers

PRAISE FOR

The Drama of the Mother-Child Bond

"This book taught me everything my own mom didn't tell me about being a mother – I wish I had read this ten years ago! I highly recommend this important book to any parent, would-be parent, or her mentor."
—Marianna Kaufman, M.D., mother of a 2-year old

"The book addresses many important issues...and factors which may adversely affect the early psychological and total human development of our children. A prescription for women who want both a successful career and family is laid out...As an obstetrician with over 25 years of experience talking to women who had faced this dilemma...I recognize how much young women will benefit from Dr. Anbar's sage counsel and clear exposition of the choices available to them...This unique, long overdue book is a must read for a mother, teacher or friend of any young woman."
—Henry Eisenberg, M.D.

"As the mother of six children, I especially appreciate the heart you bring to your analysis of the mother-child bond...Many of our young women have skewed values because of a culture that confuses the important issues of life...I believe that your book is vital to the discussion about what it means to be a woman (and especially a mother) in America now. I think the book could be a catalyst for getting young women to reevaluate their choices...and consider motherhood, as yes, a duty to society, a responsibility for parents, but also an immense blessing for those fortunate to be mothers."
—Ann Marie Buerkle, Member of Congress

For my granddaughters
Rebecca,
Ellie,
and
Naomi
Who will read this book one day

For my grandsons
Josh
Nathaniel,
and
Yoni
Who may help others with this book

And for all young women out there
in search for
the best course for
their lives,
with love!

It does not matter what is stronger, a baby's attachment to its mother or a mother's attachment to her baby. This is an instinctive dance for life in which mother and child are the partners. The first dance that will affect the rest of a child's life, coloring all future interactions—either warming the heart or chilling it, depending on the lingering effect of that first dance . . .

—Ada Anbar

Contents

Preface

I will never forget the face of a four-year-old girl, a preschool child I worked with in California many years ago. Blonde, blue-eyed, with long curly hair, she looked tired, burdened, and really old. She had been flying on weekends from West Coast to East Coast and back, by herself (under a flight attendant's supervision), to spend some time with her father. Her life was unusually muddled. While many preschoolers have near idyllic lives, others grow under knotty conditions. I wonder how she is doing today. She is a young woman by now. Perhaps a mother of another little girl...

Throughout my long professional career of over four decades, I tried to understand children's behavior and what makes some of them more resilient than others. When I first started working, teaching primary grades kids, I soon realized that inborn temperamental traits were just a small part of the equation. Although material advantages or their want were often used to explain children's disposition, this too, I observed, was not a root cause.

So when I was offered a teaching position with emotionally disturbed children in a nearby psychiatric Rehabilitation Center, children who were removed from their home because of serious behavior problems, I decided to make a career change. A psychiatric rehabilitation center, I thought, will provide a great learning opportunity to develop keener insight into children's behavior and its root causes. Six years at that center turned out indeed to be an invaluable and great learning experience.

A few years later we moved to the United States, and my younger son started preschool, joining a model early childhood program at one of our top universities. The educational component of that center was impressive, the teachers were highly professional, the facility and specious grounds well-kept and beautiful, and I was truly taken by surprise when the boy refused to stay at that place. I could not understand his behavior. So when a teaching position was offered me there, I gladly accepted it. The working hours were convenient, and I hoped, once again, to develop better insight, this time, into my own child's behavior. Following a few weeks of teaching at that program, things indeed started to get clear, providing interesting material for my first book on early childhood education, titled *How to Choose a Nursery School.* All this occurred more than thirty years ago, and I have remained immersed in early childhood education ever since.

Increasingly, I have become more and more fascinated by these early years of childhood. My growing understanding of their importance for personal development, and their potential to either facilitate or thwart one's success throughout life, has captured my imagination. What a waste, I thought, when this potential is not developed, or is mishandled. How much better it is to do things right at the beginning of life than to spend time and effort to fix problems later. And so I switched my specialty again, from special education to early childhood education.

The years between birth and kindergarten are the most critical period for human development. These years form the foundation for one's character, mental ability, and physical and emotional make up. They also require the most significant amount of adult attention—in terms of nurture, stimulation, supervision, guidance, and love. The lasting effect of these few years can be dramatically improved by a deeper understanding of young children's development and their basic needs.

While substantial information has been accumulated on this topic in the last few decades, not all of it has reached the public. Some facts are not being reported often enough to be absorbed by parents and parents-to-be and thus they get lost. Other data are occasionally misinterpreted. Certain pertinent information is suppressed and buried for political reasons, and new information continuously comes out.

And yet we live at a time when parents are required to deal with a host of issues that did not exist before the 1960s. America

PREFACE

has experienced in recent decades waves of social unrest which have
led to significant transformations in the traditional American family and the maternal role, and these shifts created drastic changes in
childcare. Many of these changes have lifelong implications for the
children, and cause a great deal of inner conflict, guilt-feelings, and
confusion among young parents and parents-to-be. Folks want to be
good parents, but they are often only partially informed, and have no
authoritative model to follow. There is a pressing need therefore, for
honest, knowledgeable clarification of issues, and fresh advice about
early childcare and motherhood; and most important about how best
to balance young children's needs with the needs of their mothers.
The purpose of *The Drama of the Mother-Child Bond* is to fill the
gaps in this much-needed information.

American society used to be fairly balanced. There was an accepted
basic social structure. Most people knew their expected function, and
their personal and social responsibility. Unfortunately, this sense of
balance has eroded. A fog of confusion has settled in, palpable among
the young as well as the old. And it is felt most intensely around issues
of childcare. There is no direction. The nation is drifting like a boat
with no one at the helm—floating in three hundred million directions.
Too often, people are making critical childcare decisions, which have
lifelong implications, with little reflection, guidance, or planning.

Yet it behooves us to give the issues of early childhood care
and education serious thought and consideration. These early years
establish the foundation for people's character and lifelong abilities. Not only is the future life of individual children at stake; but
so is the character and fate of this nation. For after all is said and
done, America's future will depend on how well we raise the next
generations.

More than forty years of professional experience in education
have come together in writing this book. I spent thirty years in early
childhood education (six years teaching at two university nursery
schools; five years studying toward my doctorate in early childhood;

twenty years of training early childhood teachers at the Graduate School of Education of the University at Buffalo; and authoring parenting books. My long experience in marriage, raising two successful sons, and observing the development of six grandchildren, while being a working mom or sometimes a stay-at-home mom, have added to my sensitivity and capability to write *The Drama of the Mother-Child Bond.*

My unique experience gives me the insight into the complexity of the parent-child relationship; I understand the needs and capabilities of young children, as well as the needs and aspirations of mothers and mothers-to-be. I know the conflict that may exist between the two. I lived it. And I have much to say about it, including a new idea how to minimize this painful, often destructive ambivalence. No other available book examines the bond between a mother and her young preschool child at that depth and from my professional background. No other book addresses issues relating to young children's development while sensitively elucidating also topics concerning contemporary motherhood. And no other book addresses with equal passion the needs of both sides in the drama of early childhood, offering an innovative transformational solution for the motherhood-career conflict.

When I first started to write *The Drama of the Mother-Child Bond,* my plan was to clarify the basic needs of young children during the early formative years. I wanted to explain what kind of early environment could best facilitate children's healthy and happy development. Of special interest was my investigation of how extended non maternal care of preschool children will affect the kids and their ability for attachment. Yet the more I became immersed in the topic, the more I realized it would be shallow to omit addressing also the needs of parents, and mothers in particular, since youngsters are totally dependent on their parents. And parental needs and aspirations, especially those of mothers who continue, in most cases, to carry the major responsibility for their children's upbringing, directly affect their parenting style and the environment they provide for the kids. So as the writing of *The Drama of the Mother-Child Bond* progressed, it gradually became also a book about motherhood, and the significance of the mother-child bond.

Over my long professional career I had many opportunities to reflect about issues affecting American childcare. I thought long and hard about the relationship between love, sex, and marriage; motherhood and career; the decline in American birthrate; or, the importance of attachment; equality of the sexes, financial security of women; not to mention the effect of daycare; the consequences of divorce, stepmothers, stepfathers, single parenting, blended families; and so on and on. All these are serious issues, with multifarious points of view, that affect all women. I tried hard to understand how these issues affect also young children's development.

No one can deny women's current difficulty, especially under the current economic condition, to create a meaningful and productive life that will benefit also children's development. Surrounded as we are by so many different lifestyles and free to pick and choose from all these options, it takes real serious thinking to chart a sensible and meaningful course. And it takes strength of character to stand against social pressure (often even from one's own family members) to chart the right course. Yet the fact remains that, while many today are cynical about life, bitter about marriage, and disappointed with their kids, many others succeed in creating for themselves and their families beautiful and meaningful lives. But this takes some serious thinking and long-term planning. It does not just happen. My purpose in writing *The Drama of the Mother-Child Bond* is to discuss with you some of the important issues that affect us all, and help women at the beginning of their adult life, make informed and intelligent choices regarding children and motherhood; intelligent choices based on wise decisions that will favorably impact their entire life.

So the primary audiences for *The Drama of the Mother-Child Bond* are young adults; women (and men) at the beginning of their adult life—even as early as senior high school—raising and discussing questions they soon will face concerning their advanced education, career choice, prospective marriage, and future children. I would like to reach young people at a period in their life when all options are still open to them, and when they still have the greatest degree of control to shape their future. I would like to encourage them to take a path they truly desire, based on informed reflection and knowledge, rather than blindly follow the latest, brazen, often politically charged trend. Other audiences for *The Drama of the Mother-Child Bond* are parents, particularly mothers of teenage daughters, and grandmothers, who can find in this book a great deal of material for discussing, at home, important issues for their daughters' future. High-school counselors, social workers, psychologists, and pediatricians, could also find this book helpful for guiding students, and discuss with them topics of interest.

It needs to be emphasized that while the topics addressed in this book may interest both women and men, they apply more specifically to women—because of their biological functions and traditional maternal role. Despite all the feminists' achievements in the last decades, America's women continue to have a greater say than men about when and if to bring a child to life. Most mothers also continue to carry a greater responsibility than fathers for raising the kids, and consequently, how to raise them. For these reasons, *The Drama of the Mother-Child Bond* is more slanted toward women and their dilemmas, their responsibilities, and their concerns.

Yet I would like to underscore, as boldly as I can, the importance of fathers in their children's lives. Fathers have a critical role in their children's development, both boys and girls, at all ages. Numerous studies indicate that kids who are raised by both a father and a mother have a much better chance to reach a healthy and productive adulthood. The father-child relationship is so important that it deserves a book all by itself.

A few more final notes: While the ideas expressed in this book were developed over decades of reflection by an educator who was raising a family (yours truly) while amassing a wealth of professional experience about early childhood, I have also drawn heavily from other thinkers and researchers I have admired over the years. They are too many to name in this preface but are given full credit in the text.

Lastly, sighing in relief that the task is done, I would like you, my reader, to know that *The Drama of the Mother-Child Bond* has had a long gestation period, much longer than nine months. But it was a labor of love. I felt compelled to under-take this difficult project, thinking long and hard about the different issues I raised till reaching sensible constructive conclusions. This is not necessarily a prescriptive book. I am not telling anyone what to do or how to behave. But I do encourage you to read the entire book before jumping to your own conclusion.

I will always remember a friend of mine, a 30-something physician and new mother of a nine-month-old baby, who volunteered to read the manuscript— and almost put it away in anger, by the end of the first chapter. She got upset, she later told me, with my expressed view about a particular sensitive topic. Fortunately, she kept on reading (not wanting to disappoint me), and then had an "aha" moment. She finally understood what I meant in the first chapter. "This is a profound book", she declared when she finished reading the manuscript. "It discusses many topics I was struggling with. And it validates me," she said.

So my hope is to inspire you, my reader, rather than prescribe, perhaps provoke you, to seriously reflect on the different topics I address, and then find the healthiest balance in your life between your maternal desires and professional aspirations and needs. Once you reach that inner point of peace and find your truly desired path out of the social chaos of contemporary America, you will feel enriched, and so will be your children, your family, and the future of our nation. The following chapters are dedicated to help you find that path.

Ada Anbar
Fountain Hills, Arizona

MOTHERHOOD, CAREER, AND CHILDREN

Love is the good we all search for, and yet we have different conceptions (and misconceptions) about what it is, ambivalence about how close we want to get to it, doubts about whether we can achieve it or even deserve it.

–Robert Karen, *Becoming Attached*

What is the Problem?

Freedom is one of the most defining characteristics of American culture. Americans are so used to feeling free that they do not appreciate how much freedom they have. Compared with other nations, Americans have more freedom of expression (with no fear of reprisal), they have more freedom of movement (with no restrictions where one can live), there is freedom of religion (one can follow any religion one desires), there is economic freedom (one is free to choose practically any profession), and there is great freedom in personal life (to be married or not, have children or not, or adopt whatever lifestyle one desires).

But freedom comes at a price. And part of that price is the burden of responsibility. While Americans cherish the rights and freedom of the individual, they do not always remember that free people, all free people, also have responsibilities. A free society that does not have a responsible majority would be chaotic; promoting, in effect, the law of the jungle.

American government does not interfere much in ones private life, and it has little to say about personal matters. This is clearly evident when one considers the topic of early childhood care and education.

We have the freedom to create for our children any early childhood environment we desire. But implicit in this freedom is the parental responsibility to establish an environment that will encourage the healthy development of the children.

Unfortunately, many folks today feel burdened by this responsibility. Many are confused by all the options that are available to them. Others give priority to personal obligations or interests, saying they are doing their best. Overall, people do not give much thought to how the early childhood environment they provide will affect their children's long term development; or how their chosen lifestyle will impact the kids. Yet one simple question needs to be asked again and again: Does a correlation exist between a child's early environment and the social/emotional and mental make-up of that child as an adult? Does it matter how we raise our children in the early years of life? Is there one early environment that is better than another? This is an important question, but people rarely ask that question today. It is value-laden, and a highly sensitive topic in our contemporary multicultural and relativistic society.

And yet, we have today ample evidence from research and observation to say unambiguously that a strong correlation does exist between children's early environment and their social/emotional and mental make-up as adults. The newly emerging science of epigenetic has also recently published hard scientific data adding strong support to this statement.[1]

Moreover, it is important to remember that parents' childcare choices affect not only one's family, but also the public at large. Americans are not used to think in these terms. We cherish our individual rights and personal freedom, and we are inclined therefore, to be self-centered. But no one can deny that the nation's future depends on how well we raise our kids. So if we have the freedom to raise them as we wish, greater thought and consideration needs to be given to how to do this job well. In the free American society, this consideration ought to be given not only by our politicians and the educational elite, but also by the majority of America's mothers and fathers.

Freedom and Responsibility

So here we are, dealing with these very issues: What is the best way to raise our young children? Who is the most qualified to do the job? And which environment is the most conducive to develop our children, the future American citizens? These questions raise the issue of freedom and responsibility.

But there is an intrinsic tension between the concepts of freedom and responsibility; There is often a conflict between parents' freedom to pursue their interests and career and their responsibility to provide a sound upbringing to their children (Some will say that these concepts represent two opposing ideals. And they do). There is a need therefore, to find a workable balance between these twin ideals; protecting the needs of children, while securing also the needs of their parents. This balance is especially important in the American society, where the individual has many options, with no outside regulation. Without such balance the nation may experience growing unrest–parents would become increasingly frustrated, children would not reach their full potential, and the nation would gradually decline.

It is odd, given the centuries-long experience that we have had with the care and education of young children, that American society still finds itself so perplexed about basic issues of childcare, confused about the most elementary aspects of the topic, and struggling without realizing, about issues of freedom versus responsibility. How many tasks are older than the task of rearing the next generation? How many functions are more important than that? We should have been experts by now, yet we find ourselves uncertain and, as Judith Warner recently put it, in a "mess." Why?

REASONS FOR THE CURRENT
CONFUSION IN CHILDCARE

Changing Conditions

There are many reasons for the current state of affairs in early child-care, and one needs to look at the problem from a broader perspective to fully understand its causes, and find a comfortable solution. Until the middle of the twentieth century, most preschool children in the United States were raised and educated at home—by their parents, another relative, a neighbor, a hired tutor, or whomever the parents would engage for that purpose. Parents were fully responsible for their young children's upbringing and education. And they made all the decisions about its nature, quality, and length. A wide discrepancy existed in kids' upbringing and a great variance in the results. Some children were highly developed while many others had a poorer upbringing. But most youngsters were given their basic needs, and were well enough prepared for the cultural requirements of the time.

But the nature of early care and education is always dependent on the culture and its values, and it is continuously being shaped by them. As societal conditions change, the needs of parents and the needs of their children also change, and so does the nature of children's upbringing. This explains why an age-long tradition of home-based early upbringing has slowly changed toward the current widespread trend of placing very young children—for part of the day, or for a full day—in center-based group care, away from home, to be raised by strangers. The reasons for this turn of events are rooted in the dramatic changes that have taken place in the American culture during the twentieth century. Let us take a brief look at some of these events.

Technological Innovations

To begin with, many technological innovations that were developed during the twentieth century revolutionized home and family management. A major outcome of these innovations was a significant reduction of labor that increased the amount of free time that became available to women compared with the past. Imagine how much time is saved in household chores since the invention of the electric washing machine (1906) and the electric tumble dryer (1915), the refrigerator (in the 1920s), the dishwasher (in 1940), frozen food products (1923), commercially prepared baby foods (1927), disposable diapers (in the 1950s), and no less important, the availability of so many ready-to-wear clothing items at affordable cost. Common to all these innovations is their time-saving factor and the significant reduction in home-based labor that is now required by a family to provide its basic needs. There is no doubt that these technological innovations have dramatically altered women's lives.

New Demographics

This all sounds good. But there was a catch. These inventions happened to take place at a period when other significant changes were also occurring. They accompanied great demographic changes associated with America's transition from rural to urban to suburban lifestyles; they coincided with the transition from life in extended families to life in a nuclear family. They occurred during a period of growing access to higher education for both, men and women, the trend to smaller families, and later on to the popular use of birth control pills—all taking place in the twentieth century. (A more in-depth analysis of these factors is presented in chapter 6.)

The New Home Economy

The end result of all these developments was a dramatic change in societal conditions. Yet while everybody was affected, women were especially affected, and in more fundamental ways. With fewer children to raise and no need to grow their own produce, rear their poultry and meat, and bake the daily bread, and with machines doing the laundry and dishes, household chores became much lighter. Home management required significantly less time and effort compared with the past. And middle-class women found themselves with more free time on their hands.

In addition, the new means of communication and transportation that were being developed—radio, telephone, television, cars, airplanes—expanded people's horizons. The greater access to higher education which spread following World War II, among both men and women, generated new employment opportunities away from home–many of which were physically not demanding and easy for women to take up. No wonder that a wave of unrest soon washed over the land. No wonder that growing numbers of women started feeling unsettled, unfulfilled, and increasingly depressed in their traditional narrow homebound role. And many started dreaming about ways to get out.

The Women's Liberation Movement

Ironically, there was an underlying paradox in this entirely new situation. As women's lives became physically easier, their emotional life became more complex and difficult. While the incentive for many of the technological innovations described above was to improve women's lives and lighten home management (in addition, of course, to the economic incentive), as household management became lighter, women grew more restless. Adjustments needed to be made to the new conditions. And it is not surprising that the women's "liberation" movement came roaring along, intending to help women find their way in this new environment. (The movement reached its high crescendo between the 1960s through the 1980s, and has been faltering since then.)

With the encouragement, even pressure, of that movement, women started taking on new social roles that often pulled them away from home. Gradually they began to shed long-standing traditions—including traditions that supported the very foundation of the social structure—shaking along the way the stability of marriage and the custom of home-based care and education of the very young. Embracing the 1960s calls for freedom and equality of the sexes, the movement also contributed to America's changing view about love and sex, often confusing the two—an important topic that will be further developed in later chapters.

Some blame the new economy for the recent changes in childcare, saying it takes two salaries today to pay the family bills, and that this reality forces large numbers of mothers with young children to work outside their home. (The rise in single-parent homes which has ballooned since the 1980s has no doubt contributed to the hardships in the new economy.) But others, as for example, human rights advocates, support the demands of the women's movement based on ideological reasons, calling for the equality of the sexes—in education, employment opportunity, home management, the law, the military, and, of course, childcare. The end result of all these demands is a deeply affected American motherhood, with a changing nature and roles.

A New Early Childhood Environment

All this development impacted, of course, young children's environment, including their care and early education. Gradually, from being fully responsible or making some arrangement with a relative, a neighbor, or a tutor (as was the custom until the mid-twentieth century), working moms began increasingly to rely on an outside agency, sometimes the government, to help raise their kids. With the growing popularity of psychology since the beginning of the twentieth century, and greater awareness of the importance of the early years of life for children's development, nursery schools, preschools, and lately daycare centers, became increasingly fashionable. Today many youngsters spend a great amount of time, compared with the past, away from their home, under non-parental supervision and care. (Many also spend too much time glued to an electronic screen, munching on sugary snacks and getting fat. Childhood diabetes has become a new epidemic in this country.)

The Struggle beneath the Surface

Sadly, the topic of early care and education has become politically charged. It is now so charged that it has turned into a political war zone. An undeclared, uneven battle is going on, and the battleground is covered by the fog of war.

As incredible as it may sound, the main opponents in this ongoing battle are parents, especially mothers, standing on one side, while children are on the opposite side. Each side is buttressed by interest groups that are rooting and advocating for it. The feminists are rooting for working moms, calling for more government intervention to establish quality programs that will help parents with the care and education of their preschool children. "It takes a village to raise a child," famously declared Hillary Clinton. The other side is supported by child psychologist, psychiatrists, and pediatricians, rooting for stay-at-home moms, and crying out loudly about the lasting damage done to children who are separated too early from their parents, and cared for by other adults.

Preschool teachers and their staff are somewhere in the middle, trying to do a balancing act between what's good for the children, while serving also the needs of their parents. Moreover, eager to create more job opportunities for the early childhood profession, and to be "politically correct," they often emphasize the needs of poor and at-risk children, while ignoring, even suppressing, what is best for the average child. Our politicians, always happy to join the fray and cater to a voting public, are inclined to support the vocal feminist groups over voiceless children. Since children do not vote, why anger their parents?

And so we find the feminists relentlessly pushing for more family-friendly legislation. Pressuring the work front for an ever larger piece of the pie, they drive more women to "break the glass ceiling." Any woman who achieves a high professional position becomes a cause celebre. Early childcare and education professionals push for, and excitedly wait for the continuously promised increases in state and federal financial support to help them with the growing demand for their public sponsored programs; growing because of the mountains of data pointing to the critical importance of the early years for children's development.

So now new questions are being raised; questions that were never asked before: Who should actually be responsible for the care and education of the very young? Is it the parents or the "village"? Who should be responsible for stimulating the latent intellectual potential of preschool children? Is it parents or preschool teachers? And who can best arouse and develop in young children—infants, toddlers, and preschoolers—their feelings and capacity for love? Is it mothers and fathers or can some parental substitute do this just as well?

The New American Reality

Inadvertently, the changing conditions in American home life since the 1960s left deep psychological scars on the American psyche. A climate of restlessness, pressure, and confusion, spread across the land, first among women, and then from them to men. This air of unrest was a hotbed for a host of new social phenomena such as widespread divorce, rising numbers of single-parent homes, teenage mothers, drug and substance abuse, and crime, all flaring up since the 1980s. The resulting cultural landscape today looks very different from the social scene of the pre-1970s. And this new reality continues to breed chains of new difficulties, increasingly requiring more complex solutions for women and children, and raising ever new questions.

For example, can one effectively combine motherhood with a career? Does being home with a preschooler mean poverty and boredom? Are working moms happier than stay-at-home moms? Should professional women take leave from their jobs to stay home with a newborn baby for a few years, or leave the child with a relative, a nanny, or a daycare provider? Can a stay-at-home mom maintain her own identity? What is the best age to become a mother? And what about the father factor, should contemporary men expect mothers of young children to work outside the home? Will they support mothers who stay home to care for their children? Can they financially support mothers today on a single salary? And with the current prevalence of divorce, can a woman rely on a husband's support? And so on and on they ask.

How do children fare under these new conditions? The next two chapters give the answer. Suffice it to say here that children do not usually ask their parents personal questions, but they do suffer. Most of the time they suffer quietly, but sometimes they will express their pain in explosive rage.

Parents Have Choices, Children Do Not

It must be noted however, that while women's childcare dilemmas are real, one ought to be fair and admit that when she becomes a mom, and weighs her needs and desires against the needs of her child(ren), the scale must be tipped as much as possible in favor of the children. It is true that women have much to give up when they become mothers, but they also have much to gain from the experience of motherhood, and it was their choice to begin with. Parents can plan ahead (indeed they ought to) and choose what's best for them and for their children from all the available options. Children, on the other hand, are totally dependent on the decisions of their parents. In an ideal world, responsible adults should not have children before they are ready and able to care for them. And once they become parents, they should arrange their life around their family responsibilities, especially during the children's early formative years.

It may sound harsh, but we need to face and debate our societal problems honestly. It is disingenuous to say that young adults cannot control their sexual drive, or fecundity, and are therefore having kids when they are not yet ready (able and willing) to care for them. Sexual behavior throughout history and culture has been shaped by cultural values. And while there always was a minority of people who rejected or rebelled against these norms, the majority did follow their culture's norms. (We all know of cultures existing today that even put to death women who transgress their culture's sexual norms.)

As for the argument that mothers of infants and toddlers need to work today for economic reasons, because they are single parents, or their husband's wages are insufficient to pay the bills, this too is often a matter of values more than an absolute necessity. To be a single mother or not, is in most cases a matter of choice. It may also be the result of irresponsible behavior. True, America is experiencing right now a difficult economic reality, and many families suffer great hardships which may require unusual arrangements. But this is in all likelihood a temporary situation. The American economy, like the economy of most other nations today, is in a state of transition. But it is fundamentally strong, and it will recover from the current hardship as it did in past generations.

It's only a Few Years

It is important to keep in mind that we are dealing here with only a few years out of a woman's sixty years of adult life—i.e. the child's formative preschool years—that should ideally be devoted to attentive mothering. This is a small price to pay for having well-developed and healthy children and a more robust society in the future. Folks can start life modestly, on one parent's salary, and upgrade their standard of living later on, when their kids go to school.

So it is moms' and dads' responsibility to make the best possible childcare choices for their young preschool children. It is their responsibility to provide the kids with the basic requirements for a healthy physical development. It is their responsibility to meet the children's basic requirements for healthy emotional and social development. And it is the parents' responsibility to create an environment that will best promote children's mental development—all key to a productive adult life. There is an abundance of information today about each of these areas of growth—some of which is discussed in later chapters—and it is the parents' responsibility to seek out this information.

Parents can of course be assisted with their childcare responsibilities by a relative, a nanny, or any other reliable person they choose. The federal government has also established a variety of programs that offer help to parents who need support with their parenting responsibilities. Communities can also provide a helping hand, organizing a variety of programs and courses that could aid parents. But there is an almost unanimous agreement among most early childhood experts that it is best when young preschool children spend the bulk of their time when they are awake with a parent. This is especially important for developing a healthy sense of attachment between parent and child—securing the bond between them and establishing a firm sense of identity. Remember, these are the Bonding Years.

A New Wave of Depression

Interestingly, in spite of all the social transformations that occurred in America during the last few decades, including the many objective improvements in women's conditions, and the positive gains that were achieved by the feminists, recent literature points to a new wave of discontent, confusion, and depression among young women, especially those in the thirty-something age group.

Thirty appears to be a particularly sensitive age, a milestone of sort. Many professional women who have reached that age, and do not have a husband or children, become mindful of the ticking bio-logical clock, and start feeling bitter for not having it all—children, husband, and a career—by that age. Distressed that they may be miss-ing the boat, many get depressed.

Women feel pressured by the clashing array of opinions around them, facing alone the critical decisions before them—irreversible decisions that have lifelong implications: To pursue a dream profes-sional track or be more practical and take future maternal respon-sibilities into account. Giving more time, in their twenties, to seri-ous courtship and romantic love, or focus primarily on their educa-tion and future career. To get married early, or lead a more carefree life, postponing marriage to a later date. To have children early or enjoy life without the responsibilities that motherhood entails. To have children first and then a career, or first establish a career and have children later. To pursue a competitive career or choose a more relaxed path that will afford greater flexibility with raising a family. To work part-time or not. To work for a corporation, or be self-employed; and so on and on. "We are a generation in the middle of a midlife crisis at 30," write journalists Lia Macko and Kerry Rubin in *Midlife Crisis at 30.*[2] "More women enter therapy at 30 than at any other point in their lives," they say. "The more choices women have, the more stressed they are," said Maureen Dowd in a conversation held on Politics & Culture.[3]

A Carousel and Two Tracks

The end result of all this social turmoil is a childcare and early edu-cation system that offers women the choice between a carousel and two tracks. On one track, we have bright competitive young women who were raised to do their best and excel, bursting with energy and an I-can-do-anything attitude. They strive for the most competi-tive schools, the most challenging careers, with expectations to rise and achieve. Nothing will stand in their way. They defer childbirth to after they are professionally established (until it's often too late), or use the daycare system—sometimes hire a nanny—to solve their childcare needs. Occasionally, these women may give up motherhood altogether in favor of a lucrative career.

On the other track, we have a large number of women, often just as bright, educated, and ambitious, perhaps a bit more mature and able to withstand the cultural pressure, who choose to settle for the more traditional path of marriage, motherhood, and being a stay-at-home mom—while the children are very young. These women tailor their career aspirations and needs around their family responsibilities. My own children say that this is the new trend. Others dub the ongoing bickering between the two groups of mothers the "mommy wars."

And then we have what has been recently labeled the "Carousel." Including perhaps the largest group of mothers with young children who choose to stay at home for awhile with their kids in their early formative years, trying later on to go back to work full time, and then back home again, on and off the "carousel," until they find the right workplace with the right conditions that allow for a comfortable balance between their work and family responsibilities; a balance that works best for them.

So what is a woman to do? Who should be responsible for the early care and education of young preschool children? Who is best suited to do this important work? What does it actually involve? And perhaps most important, who can best develop in children the human empathy and capacity for love? The following chapters explore the different aspects of these questions, providing answers and recommendations.

CHAPTER TWO

SIX REASONS TO HAVE CHILDREN

Life is a flame that is always burning itself out. But it catches fire again, every time a child is born

–George Bernard Shaw

Why Have Children?

Throughout human history children were regarded as important. To bear children was a woman's duty. Children were a woman's crown; and they were her insurance against disaster or old age. Being barren was considered a tragedy. "Give me children–otherwise I am dead," cried Rachel as long ago as Genesis.[1]

Yet considering the difficulties that children present today to their parents—the great responsibility associated with their upbringing, the loss of freedom, professional sacrifices, heavy financial cost, and loss in wages—many people regard the current lower birthrate as a sign of progress and a liberating feeling. For many American women, in particular during the period between the 1980s and 1990s, motherhood has become non-essential and a matter of choice. In this chapter I would like to discuss why it is important to have children despite all the difficulties associated with raising kids today.

THE IMPORTANCE OF CHILDREN

Raising the Next Generation

Children are important for a number of reasons, both personal and social. First and foremost is the obvious age-long need to create and raise the next generation. Procreation is instinctive. It is encoded in our genes. Whether imposed by God or by nature, the creation and upbringing of children has always been one of mankind's paramount activities. Up to the twentieth century, it was in fact women's primary and lifelong social function. Children were her trophy. "Be fruitful and multiply, fill the earth and subdue it"[2] has been the first biblical commandment.

Without procreation there can be no life. We are bound therefore, to generate new life in order to continue human existence. And it is only fair that those who were given the gift of life should give life in return. Can you imagine a society in which only a limited segment of the population would have the responsibility, or pleasure, of having and raising kids?

Moreover, although the world today does not suffer from a population shortage, the picture looks quite different on a national level. Some developed nations are already experiencing a serious population decline and overall aging; that is, the ratio of their older citizenry grows faster compared with their young citizenry. This condition has serious long-term implications from a social, economic, educational, medical, and military point of view, to name a few areas of national concern. Think, for example, of the swelling costs for a smaller younger generation that will need to support a growing older population, and maintain its Social Security and Medicare. The public debate of this problem has already begun, and we can observe its first steps in the current discussions of our new health care system.

The Social Glue

Another important fact to consider is that children, and the family unit that is engaged in raising them, form the nucleus of a society. It takes many years and a large number of people to actually be involved in that process, all sharing an interest in the outcome—parents, grandparents, teachers, neighbors, counselors, coaches, pediatricians, among many others. It is as though children constitute the invisible glue that holds a people together. The fewer children there are the weaker that glue, the larger their number and quality, the stronger the glue and social fabric of the culture. Since parents have an enormous impact on their children's development they can directly affect America's future. Chapter 4 discusses what parents can do to have the best outcome in raising their kids.

Seeds for a Brighter Future

Life is dynamic, set in a continuous sea of change. The inanimate world around us is also, albeit to a lesser degree, dynamic and changing. Icebergs melt, mountains crumble, villages are washed away by a storm, and new skylines are formed. All around, humankind leaves its footprint on the environment. Human behavior, decisions, and innovations thus affect the health and shape of the land. Well-developed children will have their chance to improve the human condition and its surroundings. Poorly developed children may add to human misery and world impairment. So children are the seeds for a better future. We must therefore provide the finest physical, educational, cultural, and social-emotional environment possible for our children to increases our chances for a good future. And parents are central in that effort.

Mothers and fathers affect their children's development more than any other individual or agency, either positively or negatively. By being careful when creating new life, and nurturing that life to a healthy and productive adulthood, parents can make an invaluable contribution to the regeneration of the world. For many folks this continues to be the purpose of human existence. And even highly accomplished older people often say that their children have been their most fulfilling achievement. As Daphne de Marneffe writes: "Devoting time to caring for children is not, of course, all about pleasure and good feeling. It is also grounded in a sense of meaning, morality, even aesthetics."[3] History abounds with stories of individuals who made great contributions to human welfare, and their parents' influence (or that of another close stable adult) during the early years of development was often notable.

Since each generation gets a fresh start to try and improve things on a personal, communal, national, and worldwide level, with parents having the power to affect their children's development, moms and dads can always hope for a better future. As the Indian poet Rabindranath Tagore wrote: "Every child comes with the message that God is not yet discouraged of man."

A Semblance of Immortality

Children can also give us a semblance of immortality. They are part of our being that will continue our bloodline, family name, memory, and some personal characteristics, also after we are gone. This verity helps many better cope with our inevitable death—something of us will remain behind on earth.

Moreover, a sense of loneliness is a common existential condition. Children help alleviate this feeling, warming our heart with the knowledge that we are never really alone in this world. Friends and relatives may die or move away, leaving us behind, never to be seen again. But our children will be there for the rest of our life. Our relationship with them may be good or not so good, close or not so close, but we will always know that part of us is out there.

An Anchor in the Sea of Life

Procreation involves much more than the fulfillment of an instinctive biological function, or the responsibility of raising the next generation. It includes an immeasurable number of complex emotions. Women in particular are very emotional about children. Many do not feel complete without having a child of their own—a sentiment that is not much discussed today, and perhaps not even well understood. Daphne de Marneffe argues that women's natural desire to raise and nurture their children has become a taboo topic in contemporary America. As she puts it:

If a century ago it was women's sexual desires that were unspeakable, today it is women's desire to mother that has become taboo. One hundred years of Freud and feminism have liberated women to acknowledge and explore their sexual selves, as well as their public and personal ambitions. What has remained inhibited is women's thinking about motherhood. Simplistic images of stay-at-home moms or career supermoms, along with endless debates about what is better for children, continue to obscure the profound meaning of mothering for many women, in all its chaos, complexity, and joy.[4]

John Locke, the seventeenth century English philosopher, considered the attachment between mother and child to be the only undeniable natural social bond. It is not always effective, Locke said, and it can, with effort, be suppressed, but it is always an existing force.

So although many women today are ambivalent and confused about motherhood, few things in life appear to be more meaningful and gratifying—to most—than their children; including their nurture and upbringing to a healthy productive adulthood. They may have an exciting, lucrative career, but most women (and men) seek, in addition to a career, an enduring exclusive emotional bond—a lasting connectedness—to the young human beings they have created. Nothing is more intimate, lasting, and exclusively part of you as a child of your own. And when children's basic needs are met in their early years of development, they reciprocate with a lifelong sense of bond. Children are like an anchor in the sea of life. Few human relationships, if any, are more enduring than that.

While no longer necessary to help secure the income of an average American family, or one's subsistence in old age, as was the case in past generations—on the contrary, today's children are increasingly becoming a financial burden—they continue to have an immeasurable emotional value. And although women can work

19

THE DRAMA OF THE MOTHER-CHILD BOND

outside their home practically in any field they desire, and lead stimulating, rewarding lives away from their family, many, if not most, find nothing more meaningful, rewarding, and enduring than their children. To be truly fully engaged in the process of life, one needs to have children.

Children's Humanizing Effect

Yet the most important reason why it is desirable to have children is perhaps their humanizing effect on us. Children keep us on our toes, helping us grow and develop and become the best we can be. Adults are continuously being shaped and braced from two sides. On the one side, we are shaped by our parents, following their model throughout life, or rebelling against it. On the other side, we feel accountable to our children. Knowing that they observe us and continuously judge us, either emulating or rebelling against us, we try our best to be a good model to them. Or at least we should. Children thus help us become better human beings, less selfish and egocentric, more giving and willing to grow and develop, as we face the many challenges they throw at us as they go through their own process of growth and development.

I share Amy and Leon Kass' view when they say that: "Marriage and procreation are. . . at the heart of a serious and flourishing human life, if not for everyone at least for the vast majority. . . . Life becomes truly serious when we become responsible for the lives of others . . . . A childless and grand childless old age is a sadness and a deprivation, even when it is a price willingly paid by couples who deliberately do not procreate."[5] Imagine the sad picture of folks at an advanced old age, lonely and frail, with no children or grandchildren who come to visit, or care for them. So permit me to end this section with a few emotional lines of my own:

Who is not touched by the sweetness of babies?
the roaring laughter of young children,
the purity of their soul,

the innocence in their eyes,
and yes, don't forget, their blind trust in us, adults.

What mother is not moved
by the voice of her toddler
just beginning to talk,
crying out loud M O M M Y!

What father is not proud
to take his four-year-old son for a drive
to show him his workplace
and show-him-off to coworkers.

And what parents don't delight
watching their five-year-old catch a ball,
or waking up in the early morning to the sounds
of little fingers practicing the piano?

Despite all the problems that exist in today's world,
and the terrible abuses that some children suffer
from sick and evil adults,
children continue to be a source
of beauty and warmth in our life.

They are an earthly twinkling star
in a dark cold world.
And a world with few children
would indeed be a grim place. . .

The Caveat and the Paradox

There is a caveat, however, and a paradox in our love of children. Since procreation is instinctive, and the natural desire to have children is hormonally driven and strong, this instinct must be controlled.

Few women could raise by themselves all the children they could potentially create. This fact has been recognized from the beginning of civilization. And it is one of the reasons why procreation has been traditionally protected by myriad of customs and laws, in all cultures, throughout human history. Only responsible adults who can provide their children a good environment in which to grow and develop should ideally have children. This is especially true in the highly developed American culture, which will increasingly require a healthy, well-educated citizenry in order to prosper and remain competitive in the global market. Children who will not receive a good early foundation will have great difficulty to catch-up, compete, and become independently functioning adults.

And here lies the paradox. On the one hand, we have bright educated young women who choose to postpone motherhood by fifteen or more years or give up maternity altogether, in favor of a good education, a lucrative career, or a care free life; as Amy and Leon Kass put it: "For the first time in human history, mature women by the tens of thousands live the whole decade of their twenties—their most fertile years—entirely on their own: vulnerable and unprotected, lonely, and out of sync with their inborn nature."[6]

In addition, millions of women who are conscious of the importance of what the women's political movement has been telling them, but who instinctively also recognize the importance of motherhood (although with little knowledge of what it actually involves), are anxious and confused. Aware that there is a conflict between motherhood and much of the feminist agenda, they contemplate motherhood with awe and uncertainty. "The prospect of becoming a mother now seems to many to be a tremendous step, a total change in life style, a fearful responsibility, an impossible expense, a frightening emotional commitment," wrote Ann Dally, the British psychiatrist.[7] Many of these women postpone motherhood to some future time, until it's often too late for them to conceive. We have reached the point where we have a "crisis of motherhood," bemoans Dally.

"Why have children when motherhood is not even appreciated," remarked to me a high-powered single woman friend. "Who has the time to have kids?" recounts Maureen Dowd, Pulitzer Prize-winning columnist for the *New York Times*, about a New York publicist friend. "Just taking care of her looks is a full-time job," she writes.[8] "Is it even responsible to bring children into this dangerous and crazy world?" asked my young friend Ana, following a discussion about current world affairs. And Mary Lou, another friend who was listening to a conversation about current lower birthrates simply stated: "Women who don't want to have children are just plain selfish."

Yet on the other hand, while many bright educated women today postpone motherhood for many years, or give it up altogether, there are alarming reports of an unprecedented rise in childbirth by unmarried women, steadily rising since the late 1990s. According to an Associated press report by Mike Stobbe, of November 21, 2006, thirty seven percent of U.S. births are now out of wedlock.[9] A 2007 CDC report (Center for Disease Control) states that out of an estimated 4,266,000 total births in 2006, the number of births by unmarried women was 1,641,700 (a rise of nearly eight percent compared to 2005).[10] In other words, more than a third of American children are now born out of wedlock. This is a staggering number.

Out of Wedlock Births

While out-of-wedlock births have long been associated with teen mothers, the latest statistics include most dramatically women in their twenties, as well as older women of all age groups. The breakdown, according to the CDC report, runs as follows: non-marital birthrates for Hispanic women, in 2005, was highest, at 100.3 births per 1000, followed by black women, 67,9 births per 1000, non-Hispanic white women, 30,1 births per 1000, and Asian or Pacific Islander (API) women, 24,9 births per 1000.

Not all out-of-wedlock births imply that there is no father around, since many couples today choose to live together without marriage. These figures also do not necessarily imply poverty and lack of ability to provide children their basic physical and material needs–we all heard of affluent single women who chose to raise a child by themselves; or professional women who did not find the right guy to marry, by their thirties, perhaps did not want to get married, and decide to have a child and raise it on their own before it is too late. But the majority of out-of-wedlock births are by teen mothers, often from poor families, who become only poorer and poorer with the birth of each child.

What is especially worrisome is that out-of-wedlock births are often condoned by today's society. While it used to be a source of shame, a stigma, just a few short decades ago, it is now accepted among single professional middle-class women who can support a child by themselves, or will move back with their parents to benefit from their material and practical support. Out-of-wedlock pregnancies are also proudly paraded by Hollywood actresses and other public and not-so-public figures.

Consider how among inner city black boys it has become a matter of status to father a child out-of-wedlock—a sign of macho to be a father before finishing high-school. "By graduation time the boys brag about how many children they have fathered," told me an inner city teacher. "I cannot counsel teen girls not to get pregnant, when their culture (the Hispanic culture, in this case) permits pregnancy at age fifteen," related another school-counselor friend. "It would be interfering in their culture, and I am not supposed to do that," she said. "You know that my friends (who were often doing drugs and engaging in promiscuous sex) laugh at you, the middle-class," confided one of my black graduate students. "They say that they are having the fun while you are working hard and paying the bills."

This lax attitude to out of wedlock births is considered to be the worst in Southern California. "Nearly half of the children born to Hispanic mothers in the U.S. are born out of wedlock," writes Heather MacDonald, in "Hispanic Family Values?"[11] "It's considered almost a badge of honor for a young girl to have a baby," says Peggy Schulze of an adoption agency in Fresno, California.[12] The fathers, of whatever age, normally take off, says Amanda Gan, director of operations for Toby's House, a maternity home in Dana Point, California.[13] "The father may already be married or in prison or doing drugs," she explains.

It is important to recognize that the prevalence of single parenting among Hispanics (or for that matter among any other ethnic group) is contributing to their inevitable slide into the welfare system. "It has become 'culturally okay' for Hispanic population to use the shelter and welfare system," says Amy Braun, who works for a home for young single mothers in crisis, in Orange County, California.[14] Given what psychologists, sociologists, and educators now know about the much higher likelihood of social pathology among children who grow up in single-parent households, we can expect the current rise in out-of-wedlock births to produce more juvenile delinquents, more school failure, more welfare use, and more teen pregnancy in the future. This permissive cultural attitude leads to unnecessary personal tragedies, a burden on the American economy, and a slow deterioration of the American culture.

Children Need Both a Father and a Mother

In summary, both mothers and fathers are needed to nurture children's physical, social, emotional, and mental development, and establish a secure sense of attachment. Fathers are essential, in addition to their financial support, for providing a male role model for boys, and, girls. They are needed to help with disciplining the children, and provide a measure of balance to the mother. Their presence is also important for overall tempering the intensity of the mother-child relationship when the child needs to become independent. As T. Berry Brazelton, the renowned pediatrician sums it: "Studies show that fathers who are available to their children expand their horizons—there are two important adults for children to identify with instead of just one. A father's involvement contributes to more stable family support for the child. . . . Father involvement gives the adolescent a surer sense of her own values and improves her ability to resist peer pressure."[15] So it is important to recognize America's problem with single-parent families and openly address the issue, on a national level, to find ways to ameliorate the situation.

The world today is more dangerous and complex than ever before. Means of destruction are more abundant and lethal than ever. Earning a decent living requires a good education and a set of specific skills. Muscle power is no longer enough for supporting a family financially, as was possible until just a few decades ago. Well-developed brain power will now be required for the individual as well as the nation, to succeed in this age of information, and overcome the dangers, including the enemies we face. The future of America depends on the quality of its people, which hinges on the environment in which they grow and develop. The alarming statistics of out-of-wedlock births poses a serious problem for the individuals and a threat to the nation. The gravity of the situation cannot be overstated, and it must be recognized and addressed.

On a Positive Note

I would like to end this chapter on a positive note. While the search for the golden path between maternal responsibilities and life-style choices and career continuous (this search will probably always be there, in some measure), more women appear to be returning to romance and marriage. According to Maureen Dowd, there seems to be a greater desire to make marriage work. As she observes, "In a world where many women either get divorced or never get married, it is now a status symbol to snag a married name . . . . Nowadays, most young brides want to take their husbands' names and brag on the moniker Mrs., a brand that proclaims you belong to him. T-shirts with Mrs. emblazoned in sequins or sparkly beads are popular wedding shower gifts."[16]

Journalists Lia Macko and Kerry Rubin write that: "It didn't take a French waiter's insults or a husband's loneliness to make either of us realize that the nonnegotiable demands of work were interfering with the nonnegotiable and much more important demands of being a friend, wife, daughter, and woman."[17] And "A remarkably high percentage of Gen-X mothers are quitting their jobs to stay at home with their kids. The 2000 census reported that 30- to 35-year old college-educated women have sparked the largest exodus of working mothers from the workplace since 1976," add Macko and Rubin.[18]

Despite their trepidation, it appears that the majority of American women now want to have children. While Douglas and Michaels lament and deride mothers' current exodus from the workplace, and the lavish attention they are giving their kids, dubbing it the "new momism;" and Judith Warner portrays current American motherhood as "perfect madness" and "a mess"; Leslie Morgan Steiner offers a more balanced portrayal of twenty-first-century American motherhood. Saying that some women are happy with their choices and some are not so happy, concluding that whether to work or not after having kids is a profound choice that splits women into two camps that disparage each other. "It's clear to me now that comparing myself to other moms is pointless; It's also clear that other moms' choices suit them and my choices are (mostly) right for me and my kids."[19] I suppose that this will always be the case.

It is also clear that if we want America to continue to develop and flourish, we need a healthy birthrate, of at least 2.1 children per woman, and provide our children the finest physical, socio-emotional, educational, and home environment possible—especially in the early formative and bonding years. The future of the nation is literally in the hands of mothers and fathers!

CHAPTER THREE

THE BONDING YEARS

*Since the Almighty could not be everywhere, He created moth-
ers, and. . . delegated part of His power to them.*

– **Shari Thurer,** *The Myths of Motherhood*

The Story of Attachment

The topic of attachment between mothers and their preschool children has been passionately debated in recent years among experts on
early childhood. This topic has become especially hot with the record
numbers of mothers with young children, including infants, who are
going out to work and widely use daycare. There are growing concerns that this practice may jeopardize children's development and
have a long-term negative impact on them.

So let us imagine a visit with several experts who gained insight
into early childhood development and hear what they have to say
about this topic. There is no better point to begin than with the
work of John Bowlby, the British pioneer of Attachment Theory, a
psychiatrist and leading researcher of personality development, and
mental health consultant to the World Health Organization, who
spent a lifetime (the second half of the twentieth century) studying
the significance of attachment between mothers and their infants and
young children.

As Bowlby was observing children who were temporarily separated from their mothers—first in a home for maladjusted boys,
then, during World War II, kids who were sent to the countryside
to escape the German blitzkrieg—he was struck by the debilitating
effect that these separations had on the children. Agonizing about
what he saw, he began a half-century-long study of the mother-child

relationship, and launched his life-long campaign for the protection of the mother-child bond during the early years of life.

Bowlby has authored several books on the topic, including a classic trilogy titled *Attachment and Loss*,[1] in which he developed his theory of attachment—elaborating on the need to establish a secure sense of attachment between young children and their mothers, and discussing the lifelong damage that may occur when such attachment is not formed. Drawing on animal studies and evolutionary biology, two fields that were developing at the time, Bowlby argued that attachment is biologically driven and is based on a desire for proximity to the mother, which increases the child's protection and likelihood of survival. Bowlby concluded that attachment is central to human survival like food and reproduction. (He focused primarily on the mother-child bond but in later years conceded that the father or another stable primary figure could also fill that role.) Following is an excerpt from an address Bowlby gave at a parenting conference, held in Chicago, in 1980:

Because successful parenting is a principal key to the mental health of the next generation, we need to know all we can both about its nature and about the manifold social and psychological conditions that influence its development for better or worse. To be a successful parent means a lot of very hard work . . . even if the load lightens a little as children get older, if they are to flourish they still require a lot of time and attention. For many people today these are unpalatable truths. Giving time and attention to children means sacrificing other interests and other activities . . . . In most societies throughout the world these facts have been, and still are, taken for granted and the society organized accordingly. Paradoxically it has taken the world's richest societies to ignore these basic facts. Man and woman power devoted to the production of material goods count a plus in all our economic indices. Man and woman power devoted to the homes does not count at all. We have created a topsy-turvy world.[2]

Bowlby's words of 1980 are just as meaningful today.

Secure Attachment

For many years, Bowlby's work was controversial. People had a hard time accepting the notion that the mother-child bond is so fragile; that its strength depends on the mother's attitude and behavior toward her child; and that its quality may affect the child's future development. (Remember, motherhood used to be revered through most of human history, to be challenged only in recent years.) But Bowlby's ideas were given a boost in the 1960s by the work of Mary Ainsworth, a Canadian psychologist who had previously worked with him in London for several years and shared his views. When Ainsworth moved to Johns Hopkins University she confirmed Bowlby's theoretical work in a clinical study, validating his ideas. And she too declared that a secure attachment between infant and mother is indeed important for the child's future development. Moreover, Ainsworth elaborated that a specific style of mothering—warm, sensitive, responsive, and dependable—is key in bringing about the positive development of kids. Based on her research, Ainsworth concluded that close to one third of middle-class American children suffer from insecure attachment, which may lead to a variety of psychological problems.

Ainsworth's work was seminal. She attracted many students to her lab, and the concept of attachment started to receive substantial attention in departments of developmental psychology in American universities. The topic was stirring heated debates among researchers, in particular in light of the growing popularity, at the time, of daycare centers. "If you put a baby in substitute care for more than twenty hours a week," warned Jay Belsky, a well-known attachment researcher, then at Pennsylvania State University, "you invoke the risk that the child will become anxiously attached, skewing all future relationships."[3]

Attachment and Love

Robert Karen is another clinical psychologist who shares Bowlby and Ainsworth's views, and has been interested for a long time in how first relationships shape a person's ability to love as an adult. In a book titled *Becoming Attached*, Karen explains that the concept of "attachment" encompasses both the quality and the strength of the parent-child bond, and that the theory of attachment is actually a theory of love and its central place in human life. "Most infants, in order to feel that their love is reciprocated, that they are valued and accepted, and that they are secure enough to happily explore the world, seem to need a lot of unhurried time with at least one person who is steadily there for them—preferably. . .with someone who is crazy about them," writes Karen.[4]

And he warns that: "Modern society has taken many of us a long way from a life centered on the pleasures and pains of being connected to others. Our focus is often on other things—achievement, power, acquisition, romance, excitement. But the need for proximity, for felt security, for love; the need to be held, to be understood, to work through our losses; these basic themes of attachment are to some degree built into us biologically. We have mixed feelings about them. But they are there."[5]

Children without Conscience

Alarmed by the radical changes in American child-rearing environment that had swept the country since the 1970s—the high rate of divorce, single-parent homes, the rising use of daycare, teenage parenting, drug use, and so forth—Ken Magid, the chief of psychological services at Golden Medical Clinic, in Golden, Colorado, wrote with Carole McKelvey a book titled *High Risk: Children without a Conscience* (1987). He was troubled by the growing number of children "without conscience" who were brought to his attention, observing that these children were emotionally unattached, and that they would hurt others without remorse. His book offers sobering case histories, illustrating the causes for these children's pathological development, and a warning to the American public to take notice. Following are excerpts from the scathing, and what appears today to be his prophetic conclusion:

> Based on extensive scientific data, the prognosis for the future includes the high probability that greater numbers of psychopathic individuals are headed our way. ... Unknowingly we may be creating a society in which more and more people without conscience will victimize the innocent. This book is about the reasons behind this phenomenon and answers the questions "why" and "Why now." The problem starts at the beginning of life, when the scales are tipped toward a future of trust and love, or one of mistrust and deep-seated rage. The critical factor is bonding. Without effective bonding the infant won't become attached to his or her primary care-giver, the mother and/or father. ... A demographic revolution is occurring which may result in future generations that have a huge number of detached children. Factors responsible include: the increasing numbers of mothers working outside the home, the child-care crisis, the teen-pregnancy epidemic, a high divorce rate, increasing child abuse and neglect, the shambles of the foster-care system, and too late adoption. All of the above, unless handled very carefully, can cause the vital attachment process to become derailed.[6]

Dead Mothers

Yet the situation is even bleaker, according to Lawrence Hedges, another mental health expert and founding director of the Newport Psychoanalytic Institute, in Tustin, California. Also Hedges is concerned about the mother-child bond in infancy and its effect on adult life. As he puts it in his 1994 book *In Search of the Lost Mother of Infancy*: "We each had a mother with whom we once shared body chemistry and bodily rhythms—primordial 'love,' as it were. Our very existence was dependent upon hers. . . ."[7] "If our development went well in terms of finding ways to connect with the psychic life and rhythms of our mother and other mothering persons—for pleasure, nurturance, and stimulation—then the first bond that characterizes human psychic love gradually forms. A dance begins in which mother and child offer to and take from each other in turn. . . this bonding dance with the mother is symbiosis. . . a mutual need-fulfilling relationship—that primordial form of merged love for which we are forever searching in one way or another throughout our lives. . . ."[8]

And Hedges warns that if many attempts to connect with mother fail, "when joyful loving is not found or re-found, or when painful neglect or rejection is experienced in infancy, an important potential for love and development is arrested, blocked, foreclosed from further development."[9] From the infant's point of view, it is as if the mother is lost or is dead, says Hedges.

Also this mental expert is concerned that with two working parents, crucial connections in infancy will fail to be made at the time, and in ways, that the infant needs. This situation will give rise to more internalized experiences of failed and ruptured connections and of "dead mothers." And like Bowlby, Ainsworth, Belsky, Karen, Magid, and others, Hedges warns that when these children grow up, they may experience difficulties in forming meaningful and lasting emotional connections with other adults.

The Daycare Dilemma

Sadly, at about the same time that important insight was gained into the significance of a secure attachment between infants and their mothers (or a substitute adult), a growing number of mothers of young children began to work outside the home. The Women's

Liberation Movement was raging, and urging women to find paid work opportunities outside the home. Women's rights issues were raised with strong political overtones. And the tenor of the feminists' demands, unfortunately, was much louder and deafening than the calls of children's advocates to protect young children's needs.

And so the idea of daycare gained growing publicity. Advocating women's "freedom" from childcare responsibilities, to enable "true equality" with men, the use of daycare became increasingly popular. "From its earliest days, the women's movement wanted to collectivize the nurturing of children and quite openly admitted the transformative possibilities of such a regime," writes Kate O'Beirne, the Washington editor of *National Review*, in 2005.[10] But the institutional group care of young preschoolers was increasingly accepted by parents from all socioeconomic levels as a good solution for their childcare needs. And so the daycare business was booming.

Soon, a long list of publications appeared on the topic. Most of these emphasized the positive aspects of daycare, aiming to allay parental concerns about leaving infants and young children in group-care situations away from home. One of the most influential of these books was *Mother Care Other Care* by Sandra Scarr, a professor of psychology at the University of Virginia, and herself a mother of four children. Published in 1984 to rave reviews, this book was considered "the first authoritative guide to child care decisions that takes into account both the child's needs and the working mother's dilemmas."[11]

Challenging Bowlby and Ainsworth, Scarr declared that "working mothers have been tyrannized by the view that the mother–child relationship is uniquely important and that its disruption is potentially ruinous for the child" (book's jacket). In later years Scarr even asserted that "multiple attachments to others will become the ideal." Shyness and exclusive maternal attachment will be seen as dysfunctional. New treatments will be developed for children with "exclusive maternal attachments" (dubbed the EMA syndrome), as reported by Kate O'Beirne.[12] And so *Mother Care Other Care* offered much support to parents who felt comfortable with the idea of daycare. The book was warmly endorsed by leading feminists, being so strongly supportive of their political agenda.

Only a few critical books were published on the issue of daycare at that time. It was not politically correct to do so. And most publishers would not risk negative reviews; As Robert Karen writes: "Certain truths do not get spoken if they seem to violate correct thinking."[13]

One rare and honest critique, published in 1983, was a poignant little book titled *The Day Care Decision*, by William and Wendy Dreskin, a husband-and-wife team. In this book, the two former enthusiastic directors of a daycare center and preschool recount their personal sad experience with daycare, and how following five years in the business and seeing additional evidence in published research, they decided to close their daycare center and move on to another profession. The Dreskins could no longer tolerate, they say, to observe the damage caused to children in their care because of the daylong separation from their parents:

We saw the differences between the children who still came for only half a day for preschool and the children who attended full time. After a year and a half of seeing this, we could no longer bear to watch. It was obvious that the children did not feel that staff-given understanding and comforting were adequate compensation for spending forty or fifty hours a week away from their parents. We found ourselves talking the center out of business, telling parents inquiring about the program that they should try if possible to work part time until the children were older."[14]

Although well written, passionate and riveting read, including important information about a critical topic, *The Day Care Decision* received little publicity. The press did not cover the book, and it was barely noticed by the public. Politically incorrect, it was soon drowned by the high waves and roaring sounds of the mothers-to-work movement. While evidence from ongoing research continued to be mostly negative, proponents of daycare relentlessly argued that it is only a matter of funding, and that if more money was allocated childcare centers could provide top-quality programs to all children—and in many cases, be even better than home care.

And so daycare advocates incessantly call on national and state administrations, and on the business community, to increase funding. Meanwhile, the childcare establishment (reportedly an industry of $36 billion a year) is now suspect, according to Kate O'Beirne, that it "has engaged in deceit and censorship to prevent an honest assessment of what decades of research can now tell us about the effect of substitute care on children."[15] (A full discussion of this topic and the results of a large scale study on the effects of daycare upbringing on children, published in 2005, is presented in chapter 5.)

As for the media's responsibility to inform the public and disseminate the truth, Journalist Bernard Goldberg, who resigned from CBS after decades of service, explains: "America's news-rooms are filled with women who drop their kids off somewhere before they go to work or leave them at home with a nanny. These journalists are not just defending working mothers—they are defending themselves."[16] And so the American public, including young mothers, remains misinformed, confused, and conflicted.

Who Is a Good Mother?

And now comes Shari L. Thurer, a psychiatrist and author of a passionate book titled *The Myths of Motherhood*, published in 1994, adding to this confusion. In defense of American mothers, Thurer declares that "A sentimentalized image of the perfect mother casts a long, guilt-inducing shadow over real mothers' lives. Actual days on Planet Earth include few if any perfect moments, perfect children, perfectly cared for."[17]

Based on Jerome Kagan's work, a Harvard University psychologist who is one of Attachment Theory's most vocal detractors, Thurer states that children are able to get attached to multiple caretakers. Like Sandra Scarr, she maintains that a child's innate temperamental traits rather than environmental factors are the strongest predictor of later maladjustment.[18] She debunks what she considers to be patriarchal "myth after myth," claiming that the "pervasive ideal of Dr. Spock's selfless, stay-at-home mother" is a historical aberration:

"Motherhood–the way we perform mothering–is culturally derived," she says. . . . "Each society has its own mythology complete with rituals, beliefs, expectations, norms, and symbols . . . our particular idea of what constitute a good mother is only that, an idea, not an eternal verity. The good mother is reinvented as each age or society defines her anew, in its own terms, according to its own mythology."[19] The contemporary American mother, even with her extensive use of daycare, is not a worse mother than in any previous generation, declares Thurer. There is no cause for alarm, she says.

And yet the American public continues to be divided on this issue, struggling to find the golden path and right balance between family responsibilities and work. While some parents consider the daycare system to be indispensable, an absolute necessity and a good solution for their childcare needs, other parents consider daycare centers to be categorically unacceptable, "awful," and "dangerous." Nothing epitomizes better the difference between these two groups than Kate O'Beirne's statement that "debates over day care, usually dubbed 'the mommy wars' are among the most treacherous fought out in the public square."[20]

It is important to note that the mother-child (or parent-child) bond is more important today than in past generations. Living as we do in nuclear rather than extended families, this bond is a child's only secure anchor in life. And, this bond is necessary for developing self identity, self confidence, and the very motivation to strive and develop, without which children will have a hard time to become successful adults.

Throughout this decades-long dispute, Bowlby kept standing tall, never getting discouraged by the many attempts to criticize, reject, or ignore his attachment theory. He steadfastly maintained his firm belief in his theory, certain that public opinion will eventually turn around. In a 1989 interview he remarked: "Well, times change. I mean people don't smoke; they used to. I think women will realize that if they have children then they have responsibilities, and if they want to have happy relationships with their children in later life, then it's important to do a lot of work with them when they are small. But I give it another twenty years."[21]

Bowlby's statement may have been prophetic. Recent literature indicates a growing shift in the public's attitude. While the issue of attachment has been simmering for several decades, new writings indicate that the debate about it is heating up. Moreover, the circle of debaters is widening. While earlier concerns were expressed primarily by mental health experts, mostly men, new debaters include pediatricians and, increasingly, mothers. There is a new willingness by women to be politically bold and take on the feminists and their women-centered agenda, to have an honest debate on childcare issues, while keeping politics out. Before we listen to these mothers, let us listen briefly to the advice of leading pediatricians.

A Pediatrician's Advice

Parents often discuss childcare issues with their children's pediatrician. So what do pediatricians advise parents? Let us listen to Berry Brazelton, a renowned pediatrician (clinical Professor of Pediatrics Emeritus at Harvard Medical School and Professor of Pediatrics and Human Development at Brown University) and Stanley Greenspan, Clinical Professor of Psychiatry and Pediatrics at George Washigton University Medical School, both children's advocates, who wrote in 2000 *The Irreducible Needs of Children*.

Concerned that about 50 percent of America's youngsters are now reared for significant parts of the day by someone other than a parent, these two experts have joined the chorus of mental health specialists described earlier, warning that "a new type of institutional care" is evolving in America; a form of care in which fundamental requirements for a healthy childhood development are not being met.

The authors identify seven "irreducible" needs "without which children cannot grow, learn, and thrive." Chief among these is the child's need for consistent nurturing relationships. "Nurturing emotional relationships are the most crucial primary foundation for both intellectual and social growth," write the authors.[22] They wrote their book, they say, as a wake-up call for parents who care about the future of their children; a reminder to be judicious about the use of daycare.

In a follow-up book, *The Four-Thirds Solution*, published in 2001, Greenspan takes off the gloves and delves deeper into the problem of out-of-home care for young preschool children, saying that "almost 13 million infants, toddlers, and preschoolers—more than half of our nation's 21 million preschool populations—are receiving care from someone other than their parents or another family member. . . . Our society has launched into a monumental experiment that has the potential to change who we are and how we function...as recent research has shown, our societal experiment isn't going well. . . . "[23]

Like Ken Magid and Hedges, a decade earlier, Greenspan warns that:

> With two-career families, high divorce rates, many single parents, and increasing numbers of parents with more than one job, as well as fewer extended-family households, children have fewer and fewer opportunities to develop warm, close ties to the adults in their lives. As a result, there is a danger that we will see more self-centered, impulsive, or passive, and hopeless children or young adults than in the past...there

are already worrisome signs that children are struggling in this new world. The United States has the highest rate of childhood homicide, suicide, and firearms-related deaths of any of the world's 26 richest nations. The murder rate for children has tripled since 1950 . . . . Obesity among children has doubled in the last 20 years.[24]

Defying political correctness and determined to fully state the truth, Greenspan continues:

The plain, unvarnished truth is that parents struggling to raise children in the hectic, pressured world of dual-career couples, unbounded ambition, around-the-clock shift work, and nonexistent extended families often are too busy, tired, or preoccupied to give their children the time and attention that intimate relationships require . . . .They are enormously successful. They not only have busy careers, but also serve on the boards of corporations and worthwhile charitable organizations. They contribute time to community organizations. But something is missing from their very full lives—a sense of intimacy in the family. We need to shift our priorities. . . . Parents and future parents need to plan their careers and lifestyles more carefully so that they can fit in the time and attention that children need.[25] Our first priority is to get parents home with young children, even if it means fewer working parents, lower earnings for the families, and lower tax revenues because of their lower earnings," he declares.[26]

A New Message from Women

At last, we now see a growing vocal split among working moms, and a return to greater sense and sensibility. Notwithstanding mothers who absolutely need to work to support their families, countless women have been moving away from the self-centered feminist agenda, recognizing the need to change their attitudes toward motherhood and career. The generation of women that was swept off the ground by the feminist movement has had a crash landing. The movement is loosing its mystique, and the daughters of the founders, having a mind of their own, are changing their tune. I couldn't say it better than Joan Peters, author and literature teacher, in her 2001 book titled *Not Your Mother's Life.*

Interviewing women in their twenties, thirties, and early forties, to learn about their goals and life strategies, Peters was repeatedly told that they're tired of hearing how hard it was for their parents:

> They don't want to be guilted into the boomers' political agenda. They don't feel they have to prove that women can make it in a man's world. Growing up knowing that women can do whatever they want, and often as not feeling pushed to achieve, they prefer to figure out for themselves how they'll live. Not surprisingly, a lot of them reject what their female boomer bosses have: no life, no kids—or kids they never see because they're working so hard. Those women, so I have heard, can be tougher bosses than men; more exacting, never giving the younger women a break . . . ."[27]

The new generation of women wants a career and a life, says Peters. And she counsels that "every woman can design the life she wants," recounting as example, the life stories of a number of women who found a good balance for their lives.

Once Again the Most Important Job

Ann Crittenden, an award-winning economics journalist, resigned from an established and highly rewarding position at the *New York Times* to have more time with her infant son. Motherhood is the most important job one can have, she says in *The Price of Motherhood*, quoting Theodore Roosevelt's famous statement that "The good mother, the wise mother . . . is more important to the community than even the ablest man; her career is more worthy of honor and is more useful to the community than the career of any man, no matter how successful."[28]

It is unfortunate, writes Crittenden, that this important job is disrespected and devalued in today's workplace. As she puts it: "One of the worst-kept secrets of the past two decades is the quiet exodus of highly trained women from corporations and the leading professional firms," who are leaving their job once they face the lack of tolerance for women's family responsibilities. These women did not anticipate the degree to which they would fall in love with their new babies, says Crittenden.

She then gives an interesting breakdown of women's current standing in the different professions. For example, in law, "Typically, female graduates flock into the big firms, work morning, noon, and night for a few years, and then depart, leaving the fat pickings of partnership to the men . . . only 13 percent of the partners in the 1,160 largest law firms, and only about 7 percent of the equity partners, who share in a firm's profits, were women," writes Crittenden. In later years these women "are more apt to go into the relatively low paying, less pressured areas of government and legal services, and, increasingly, corporate in-house counsel; the reason is children."[29]

In science, the "woman situation" has been compared to a leaky pipe, "a roiling Amazon of smart graduate students at one end reduced to a trickle at the other. "Only a handful of female graduate students make it to tenured positions in academic science departments," says Crittenden.[30] They choose to leave the race once they have children.

"Of the 126 medical schools in the United States, fewer than 10 percent of full professors were female."[31] "Act like a man and time your pregnancies appropriately," advised a 1995 guidebook by the Harvard Women's Law Association. The price that women have paid for this advice, says Crittenden, is a high degree of childlessness. It is estimated that more than 25 percent of female college graduates of the baby-boomer generation will never have children, she writes.[32]

Among the solutions Crittenden offers are a more family-friendly workplace, encouraging communities to be more family-supportive, and pass new legislation that will enable mothers to have the time they need with their young preschoolers.

They All Wished They Had Children

And then there is Sylvia Ann Hewlett's spirited 2002 book, *Creating a Life*. An economist and founding President of *the Center for Work-Life* Policy, Hewlett interviewed powerful women in fields previously dominated by men, and was astonished to find that none of these remarkable women had children. More significantly, none of these women had *chosen* to be childless! "These highly accomplished women vaulted over barriers and crashed through glass ceilings, but found it extraordinarily difficult—if not impossible—to have children as well," she writes.[33]

They all wished they had found a way to have children. And many of them went to the ends of the Earth to find a baby, spending huge amounts of time, money, and energy. But "after age 40 only 3 to 5 percent of those who use the new assisted reproductive technologies succeed in having a child," she writes. The more successful the woman, the longer her workweek; 50 to 60 hours a week are common, leaving little time and energy to establish a family. They "can be playwrights, presidential candidates, and CEOs, but increasingly, they cannot be mothers."[34]

It is surprising, says Hewlett, that despite the fact that a significant percentage of young women experience fertility problems, 89 percent of high-achieving young women in her survey still believed they will be able to get pregnant into their forties. Women are not told the truth, she says. "Over 90 percent of late-in-life pregnancies involve IVF (in vitro fertilization) and prices range from $10,000 to $100,000, depending on how many attempts are required and whether or not you need donor eggs."[35] (A website reportedly, auctions off eggs of fashion models with opening bids ranging from

$20,000 to $150,000.) Fertility treatments also carry serious risks, says Hewlett, with the possibility of multifetal pregnancies, increased risk of cancer of the reproductive organs, and miscarriage. Women's window of fertility remains extraordinarily short and they need to deal with childbirth in a timely fashion if they want to be able to enjoy risk-free pregnancies and joyous births, concludes Hewlett.

Maternal Desire Is Central to Women's Identity

Another noteworthy factor to consider is that a mother's desire to care for her children is a central feature of many women's identity rather than an inconvenient detail, says Daphne de Marneffe in *Maternal Desire* (2005). The more connected mothers feel to their children the more "their lives make sense" to them. Placing a child in a substandard care situation makes mothers feel worse about themselves, she observed. Economic considerations are of course always there. But, as she puts it: "one sometimes gets the sense that economic 'reality' is invoked to shut us up. . . . When mothers' interests are defined solely in terms of their economic interests, it tells us less about "reality" than about values, values about money and time that define away much of what is emotionally important to actual mothers."[36]

De Marneffe is a Harvard and Berkeley educated clinical psychologist and mother of three children; admittedly a onetime feminist who felt liberated when she made the transition (after the birth of her third child) from a professional woman to becoming essentially a mother. "I was moving from a shaky endorsement of a model in which children were fitted into my previous life to a desire for a life centered on mothering, from which other priorities flowed."[37]

How could it be, she wonders, that at the dawn of the twenty-first century, the ancient imperative that women mother their children felt somehow liberating and new? . . . I couldn't bear to leave our baby; when I was away, I ached, and in her presence, I couldn't imagine a worthwhile reason for leaving her. . . ."[38]

Maternal desire is "one of the most transforming and powerful experiences in women's lives," writes Marneffe, and it should be a legitimate focus of intellectual inquiry and personal exploration. "Simplistic images of stay-at-home moms or career supermoms, along with endless debates about what is better for children, continue to obscure the profound meaning of mothering for many women, in all its chaos, complexity, and joy."[39]

A Feminist Backlash

Just as I was sighing in relief, thinking to myself, "Aha, they finally got it; healthy common sense is back," I received a new book in the mail: *The Mommy Myth*, by Susan J. Douglas, a professor of Communication Studies at the University of Michigan and Meredith W. Michaels, a Lecturer/Research Associate at Smith College. If *Maternal Desire* was penned with a heart full of love, love of children, and love of mothers (all mothers, working moms as well as stay-at-home moms), *The Mommy Myth* overflows with feelings of hate. It is a shrill feminist backlash against America's rising objections to the Women's political movement.

"Why is it that mothers, most of whom have wanted, with all their hearts, a truly decent, caring, educational childcare system in the United States, feel incredibly guilty about childcare?" ask the two authors.[40] For most mothers, work is an absolute necessity, they argue, livid about the American government's refusal to support universal childcare because, as they say, of "dumb men's stupid choices."

The two authors deride what they dub the "new momism," that is, women's decision, including professional women, to stay home with their young children and be dedicated to their care and nurture. The new momism involves more than just impossible ideals about child rearing, they say. It redefines all women, first and foremost, through their relationships to children. "The problem with the new momism is that it insists that there is one and only one way the children of America will get what they need: if mom provides it."[41]

Douglas and Michaels insist that they love their children. But they seem to equate maternal love (including the desire to protect and nurture one's youngsters) with subservience. "The new momism is not about subservience to men. It is about subservience to children," they say.[42] And "With so many smart, hard working, dedicated, tenacious, fed-up women out there, can't we all do a better job of talking back to the media that hector us all the time?" they ask.[43]

And so they challenge women to go back to a time when they felt free to tell the truth about motherhood—"that at times they felt ambivalent about it because it was so hard and yet so undervalued— and when women sought to redefine how children were raised so that it wasn't only women who pushed strollers, played Uncle Wiggly, or quit their jobs once kids arrived. Of course these women loved their kids. But were they supposed to give up everything for them? Are we?"[44]

When I finished reading Douglas and Michael's angry book I couldn't but conclude that there will never be a time in free American society when all women will be happy and at peace with their many options, responsibilities, and choices. I suppose that the conflict between motherhood and career will continue to exist and so will the search for the golden path between the two. But it appears that the tide has turned, and so have many mothers' attitude toward childcare. The point is that there is now a socially acceptable choice. And it is important to choose wisely.

While several new publications by women authors continue to lament the practical and emotional difficulties of motherhood, there is a growing understanding of the primary importance to establish a warm secure attachment between parents and children in the early years of life. There also is the recognition that the early preschool years are critical for children's development. This understanding will continue to spread as time goes on because there is so much more to clarify about this topic. In the meantime, the term "Attachment Parenting," first used in the 1980s by William Sears, the bestselling

Canadian pediatrician,[45] is slowly seeping into the culture, and we will hear much more about this in the future.

Conclusion

Thus we see how the issue of attachment has captured the attention of many early childhood experts and a growing number of mothers. One can no longer remain oblivious to the widespread concern about the recent changes in American society and their effect on the development and behavior of America's children. Many youngsters today are unable to form close attachment to their parents, and truly bond with them. These children may be potentially unable to form close relationships with others as adults. Poor attachment between parents and children is also considered by mental health experts to be a root cause for other forms of maladjustment observed in American society today. There is a growing apprehension that things will only get worse if significant improvements will not occur in family relationships, particularly in the early years of children's life. The remedy for this anxiety is more parental time spent with young children, in the first three years of life, creating a deeper bond between parents and their children.

Fortunately, more women are rediscovering the importance and joys of motherhood (while remaining cognizant of its many difficulties and required sacrifices). More women are willing to take time off from a fast career track to spend time with their infants and toddlers. And more women are becoming realistic about the demands of a professional career and the sacrifices it requires from their personal lives.

The ultimate resolution of the conflict between work and family responsibilities will continue to fall mostly on mothers, for two reasons. First, family responsibility blends best with women's biological functions. Second, if fathers were to take equal part in childcare as mothers, many would be unable to fully develop their own career, thus giving an advantage to single men and women who will have a better chance to excel, and gain higher wages and status than married people. (In individual cases, however, the gender roles between a mother and a father may be reversed, if both agree to that.) But mothers will not be able to remedy the current chaotic situation by themselves. They will need the support and understanding of their men. They also need the appreciation and support of society. This does not mean a return to the past, or a loss of women's recent social gains. It simply calls for a readjustment of attitudes, on a personal and cultural level—a point we will further discuss in the following chapters.

Different recommendations have already been proposed about how to achieve a comfortable balance between family responsibility and work, including a call on employers to redesign the workplace to better fit parental needs; create many more part-time jobs; giving every woman the right to a year's paid leave; or shortening the workweek. There are recommendations to women to make it a priority to find a husband in one's twenties, have the first child before age 35, and resume one's fast career goals only after children are in grade school. Others suggest having a 50/50 or four-thirds arrangement between mother and father; both choosing a career that enables flexibility and a workplace that supports a reasonable work/life balance; or starting an entrepreneurial work at home. (I like the term "Mompreneur," which I found in a recent *USA Today* article.) Communities are also called on to be more proactive and supportive of parents, by offering parent-education courses, support-groups for new mothers, community pediatric clinics, limited babysitting service, and so on. Chapter 7 describes my recommended cultural shift in attitudes toward the motherhood/ career conflict, offering a new paradigm for American motherhood.

Years ago, Mary Ainsworth said that, "Women's-lib people have been finding it comfortable to assume that it doesn't matter what you do and that a woman owes it to herself to work and do what fulfills her. People who focus primarily on the welfare of children tend to ignore what suits the mother. But it's really a matter of how do we adjust these two things."[46] Ainsworth's words are just as valid today.

CHAPTER FOUR

MOTHERHOOD TODAY

*Marriage and procreation are . . . at the heart of a serious
and flourishing human life, if not for everyone at least for
the vast majority. . . life becomes truly serious when we become
responsible for the lives of others.*

–Amy and Leon Kass, *Wing to Wing, Oar to Oar*

Motherhood in Perspective

Traditionally, women have been the primary caregivers of their
young children. Because of their biology, women have always been
the breeder-feeders of children. "The key is milk," says psychiatrist
and historian Shari L. Thurer.[1] Milk explains the earliest division of
labor, she says, making males the hunters and females the gather-
ers. Foraging for food was much more amenable to simultaneous
nursing than hunting. And sustained nursing gradually evolved into
childcare.

So for better or worse, from the Stone Age all the way up to
the last third of the twentieth-century, mothers were usually the
primary caregivers of their youngsters—responsible to meet the
children's needs and supervise their upbringing and education, as
limited as it may have been. As is always the case, some mothers
were probably better than others, some enjoyed motherhood more
than others, and some lived under conditions that were more conducive for good mothering. Whatever its state, a mother's role was
clearly defined. The Virgin Mary, with the loving portrayal of her
holding her baby Jesus, has been a popular icon of the Western
maternal ideal.

Customs are Changing

Customs of motherhood would vary among the different cultures and eras, meeting each society's needs, expectations, and values at a particular period. Mothers were often assisted by other women—be it a grandmother, aunt, sister, wet nurse, nanny, or teacher. But the majority of mothers throughout history were fully engaged with their youngsters' upbringing, going about their daily chores while keeping the children within their proximity, and an eye on them—unless they were very poor, unwed, or unable to take care of them. In these cases, they would give up their children for adoption, place them in foundling homes or monasteries and convents, and sometimes even kill them. (For a detailed description of the varied cultural customs—at times quite gruesome–which mothers followed at some periods and places, see *The Myths of Motherhood* by Shari L. Thurer.)

However, following the cultural shifts that occurred in the United States during the last century, what was good for Grandma may no longer be workable today. Most of us are no longer surrounded by an extended family that can pitch in and help. American mothers do not give birth anymore to ten children; many mothers choose to bottle-feed their babies; and millions of women, including married middle-class mothers of very young children, are working long hours outside the home, leaving their infants and toddlers in nonmaternal, often group-care situations.

The institutional care of very young children happened only once before in the history of mainstream America. During World War II, industrialist Henry Kaiser, who was hurriedly building ships for the military under time pressure, established childcare centers at his shipyards to enable women to join the war effort. Nearly four thousand children were served in these centers which closed by the end of the war. But the recent cultural changes have affected the nature of contemporary motherhood, making it, as British psychiatrist Ann Dally succinctly put it, "full of uncertainty and paradox, fraught with dilemmas at all stages, arousing passion and anxiety, creating illusion and also being altered by it . . . ."[2]

A contributing factor to the current complexity of motherhood is the newly acquired equality in education, and employment opportunity, between women and men. While wonderful for women, this achievement casts a shadow on many households, and childcare issues in particular, often causing gender-role confusion. Fathers are now expected to actively participate in parenting, with some folks contending that mothers' traditional nurturing role can now be provided also by men. "Fathers can also do the mothering," they say, adding to the culture's confusion. While societal roles were clearly defined until just a few decades ago, today everything has become a matter of choice. As Dally puts it: "Most people in the last century had no doubt that family life was best or that raising children was a duty to God. Now we are not so sure about the family, the children or God."[3]

Yet while poor single mothers may have no choice, other reasons must compel married middle-class mothers of preschool youngsters (sometime even infants) to go out to work full-time. Economic considerations are often given as the primary reason. But as Daphne de Marneffe writes:

> Economics are of course always central to needing to work and paying for day care. But one sometimes gets the sense that economic 'reality' is invoked to shut us up . . . . When mothers' interests are defined solely in terms of their economic interests, it tells us less about "reality" than about values, values about money and time that define away much of what is economically important to actual mothers.[4]

So what drives married mothers of very young kids, who have a working husband, to work full-time away from home? Why don't they stay home with their youngsters in the first few years of life? We discussed some of these reasons in the first chapter—an exciting career, a desire for independence, boredom, loneliness, depression, or peer pressure, for example, in addition to economics. But there seems to be another explanation; a simple explanation that may better explain mothers' change of heart from past practice. Many parents may be unaware of how critically important they are for their infants' and toddlers' development. Growing up themselves in small families, they may not know what good mothering actually involves—especially in the first two to three years of life. And they may be uninformed about the knowledge gained in the last few decades about early childhood development; a period increasingly recognized as important for its lasting impact on children's behavior and capabilities as adults.

Lacking this knowledge, and pressured by the culture to go out to work and be financially independent—while interesting lucrative alternatives, including a promising career, are beckoning all around—it should not be surprising that many mothers opt to go to work, finding nonmaternal care arrangements for their infants and toddlers.

The Preschool Years

The purpose of this chapter is to turn on the light on motherhood during the early preschool years and clarify what it involves; and what may be lost if this period is neglected. Girls can become pregnant by age twelve or thirteen and give birth to a child nine months later. From the biological standpoint they become mothers at that time. But very few folks in the United States would advocate motherhood at that early age, nor believe that such girls could become good mothers (although this is a common practice in underdeveloped countries, where people live in extended families).

In America and the rest of the developed world, motherhood involves much more then giving birth to a child, followed by a period of nursing, providing food, clothing, and shelter. Becoming a mother is one of the most profound, exhilarating, and transforming events in a woman's life. It is also one of the most demanding experiences, requiring energy, maturity, and intelligence. Women's natural desire to be good mothers involves today a host of difficult issues. And because of this difficulty motherhood is now commonly being postponed (or at least it should be) by some ten years or more—from the age of puberty to an age when women reach a higher level of personal maturity.

Let us then take a closer look at what it means to be a mother in twenty-first-century America. Why is motherhood considered today to be difficult when biologically speaking it is so easy for most girls and young women to become mothers (unless they wait past their peak fertility age, which is between ages 25 to 35 when pregnancy difficulties begin). What does America expect of its mothers? And what are a mother's actual responsibilities?

A MOTHER'S MISSION

Before the Child Is Born

A mother's responsibility begins months before her baby is born, at the prenatal period. Her behavior during the gestation period will affect the baby's physical as well as mental development for years to come. She can increase the probability of giving birth to a healthy baby, both physically and mentally, or she can increase the odds of delivering a sickly underdeveloped child, physically and mentally. Therefore, medical supervision during the pregnancy period at the doctor's office or in a prenatal clinic is very important to ensure the mother's health as well as her baby's development.

Healthy balanced nutrition with the right amount of nutritional supplements is important during pregnancy, and even for a while before that, to protect the mother's health and provide a healthy environment for the growing fetus. Evidence from the newly emerging science of epigenetics indicates that maternal nutrition can even affect a wide variety of characteristics in an offspring, including health, appearance, long term memory, and mental function.[5] So is the importance of drinking sufficient amounts of good clean water, and avoiding toxins from cigarette smoking, alcohol and substance abuse, or any other source of pollution that may contribute to an unhealthy environment. Getting enough sleep and maintaining a moderate level of exercise regime is also necessary for a healthy pregnancy.

Keep in mind that a fetus can hear in the womb and that loud unpleasant sounds may cause damage. According to the neuroscientist Lise Eliot, there is evidence that fetuses exposed to high level of noise may suffer a higher-than-average rate of permanent hearing loss. The period of greatest sensitivity to noise damage begins at six months of gestation and extends through a few months after birth.[6]

Stanley I. Greenspan, the renowned child-psychiatrist, also warns that the need for a safe and secure environment starts well before birth. As he puts it: "Many babies are put at risk before they are born. They're exposed to all kinds of assaults that endanger the growth of their nervous systems. Smoking, alcohol, and other toxic substances undermine the growth of a healthy nervous system. We're seeing more and more of the ways in which they can interfere with later ability to process sensations (sights and sounds), as well as organize thoughts."[7]

What's most important to remember, however, before any pregnancy begins, is the couple's responsibility to become pregnant only when they want to have a child, and when they are able to meet that child's basic needs. Babies are not dolls that can be tossed aside when something more exciting appears. A sense of responsibility toward them needs always to be there. As Brazelton and Greenspan put it: "Babies need to be secure in their world, and they need to be born into families who want them. Society must see that unwanted births are prevented. Information on contraception and reproductive health should be available to every woman of childbearing age."[8] When these precautions are kept before a pregnancy begins, and during the nine months of gestation, there is a good chance that a healthy, well-developed infant will be born.

WHEN ACTUAL MOTHERHOOD BEGINS

The Home Atmosphere

Once a baby is born, actual motherhood begins. And so much of it is about giving. This is when it starts getting difficult, physically and emotionally, and that is when many mothers start having problems. A mother has to be continuously on the giving side during the child's first year of life, by day and by night—giving nourishment, affection, protection, clean diapers, fresh clothing, stimulation, love, and somewhat later, structure, limits, and discipline. Moreover, with no verbal communication available to help clarify needs, a mother must be sensitive enough to feel and assess the infant's wants and capabilities at each phase of development; meeting these on an age-appropriate level, at the right measure, and at the right time. The child's father, grandmother, and other adults can of course help, but mothers are biologically and hormonally wired to be the most tuned to their babies' needs, so that this responsibility falls mostly on their shoulders. It is very helpful when a mother is content, at peace, and in love with her new child, because a baby can sense the mother's mood, and is affected by it. The infant has the greatest chance to thrive when the mother is at peace.

A mother's responsibility does not end with the baby, however. She needs to balance her special time with the baby with other responsibilities she may have—to other children, a husband, a possible job, the home, other family members, and not the least, herself, remaining in touch with her own feelings and needs. To be a first-time mother may sound like a tall order, and it is. Yet somehow, most of us manage to wade through this difficult period. There is no wonder, however, that many first-time mothers cry out for help–to their husband, mother, another family member, a babysitter, a nanny, a daycare provider, or the government.

Daphne de Marneffe, the ex-feminist scholar who finally found her inner peace after her third pregnancy when she decided to be a stay-at-home mom, wrote a long monograph on maternal desire. In this book Marneffe encourages all mothers, as much as possible, to stay home with their young infants and toddlers during the first two to three years of life, rather than giving over that responsibility to a nanny or a daycare provider. Most women have the maternal desire to raise and nurture their young children, she writes, irrespective of the practical and emotional difficulties this may entail. "Caring for young children is something mothers often view as extraordinarily important both for their children *and* for themselves," she says.[9] "Maternal desire is not, for any woman, all there is. But for many of us, it is an important part of who we are," she adds.[10] Remember also that maternal care and nurture is observed in all mammals. It is an innate behavior associated with survival. And maternal desire can be viewed essentially as an expression of love; that is maternal love.

Douglas and Michaels's derogatory view that a mother's intense desire to take care of her young child—dubbed by them as "intensive mothering," or the "new momism"—equals subservience is bizarre. As they say, "The new momism is not about subservience to men. It is about subservience to children."[11] But their feminist's sensibility must have blurred their distinction between true love, with its inherent sense of devotion, protection, and the desire to give, and subservience—which is a service provided by a subordinate.

All this does not imply that moms have to be bound to a baby twenty-four hours a day, seven days a week. The child's father can and should help. And men are indeed increasingly participating in the parenting process. Other people can also be called on to help with some of the functions—grandparents, friends, neighbors, babysitters, and later on, teachers. But it is important for one person to have the continuous overall responsibility for the child, spending the bulk of the child's up time with him or her (in the first two to three years of life), orchestrating all the child's activities. This person must be a loving and stable presence in the child's life, to promote a sense of stability, security, and belonging. And this person will slowly become the child's anchor, the root, during the critical years of development; enabling, through the process of identification, the slow emergence of self-identity. That person will also become the child's primary authority figure; the one who sets the boundaries and lays the foundation for the necessary sense of discipline.

Usually this person is the mother, with the father (sometimes someone else who is close to the child) having a supportive role. As de Marneffe writes:

> Caring for small children is compellingly central to many women's sense of themselves to a degree still not experienced by many men. . . . This may be changing . . . . But for the moment, the care of children remains a predominantly female occupation. Some argue that this is a problem in need of correction—that true equality of the sexes cannot be achieved until child rearing and work responsibility are equally shared. But whatever position one takes of this matter, and whatever one's social ideal for the division of labor, the idea that equality between men and women—or fairness between any two partners—can come about only through similar life courses and a parallel allocation of labor may constitute an abstraction by which few people actually want to live.[12]

Different solutions have been proposed how to better share the parenting responsibilities between mothers and fathers. A variety of arrangements are possible, depending on the parents' type of job, schedule, flexibility, and desire. There is the 50/50 solution, where the mother takes care of the child two and a half days a week, and the father stays with the child two and a half days, so that both parents could work part-time outside the home. Or, there is Greenspan's "Four-thirds solution," in which each parent works only two-thirds of the time, instead of full-time, so that each can devote one-third of the workweek to their child, with the two sharing childcare responsibility during the weekend.

"In some families, one parent might work half-time and the other 80 to 90 percent of the time. In another, one parent might work 40 percent of the time and the other parent could work full time. In yet another, one parent doesn't work at all for two or three years, while the other puts in mega-hours. All these alternatives may be reasonable to particular families," writes Greenspan.[13] The basic premise is that children's needs should be the chief concern in both parents' careers and financial decisions, and that the parents should have an honest conversation about their plan before they begin implementing it, ideally before they have children, in order to minimize confusion and friction.

Greenspan warns, however, that the only way a couple can have a reasonable discussion about children and childcare that won't immediately "spark a raging inferno of accusations, anger, and alarm is by changing our basic assumption." We have to approach the topic with the assumption that both parents share their parenting responsibility, their family finances, and their career aspirations, discussing how best to work toward their goals. It is also helpful to keep in mind that children can do quite well, says Greenspan, being cared for by others for a limited number of hours a day, and that we are talking only about the first two or three years of a child's life. Once the child goes to kindergarten mothers will have much more free time to pursue their own interests.

A Mother's Job Description

So what is it all about? What is a mother's actual job description? Why should a young, healthy, and energetic woman, often highly educated and professionally experienced, stay home for a few years with a new baby? What is so important about the first two to three years of life worth putting on hold a mother's own career or other personal interests?

Childcare responsibilities can be divided into three areas of development. There is the physical aspect of child growth and development, the social/ emotional aspect of child growth and development, and the mental/cognitive aspect of child growth and development. Although there is much overlap between these domains, it is easier to discuss the topic when grouped in this manner.

MOTHERHOOD AND YOUNG CHILDREN'S

Physical Development

To ensure the proper physical development of a newborn infant, assuming there was a healthy pregnancy and delivery, the baby must be provided with good nutrition, warmth, hygiene, clean air, sensory stimulation, and lots and lots of love and cuddling. Breastfeeding is considered today to be the ideal method of feeding and nurturing infants. According to the Department of Health and Human Services, "Breastfeeding is one of the most important contributors to infant health."[14] Extensive research documents that breastfeeding provides a range of benefits for infants as well as for their mothers.

Breastfeeding

A mother's milk contains the most fine-tuned combination of nutrients and micronutrients needed for a child's growth and development. It contains factors that will affect the immune system of the new infant, in addition to transmitting through her milk the mother's immunity, including some other features lasting a lifetime.

According to the Department of Health and Human Services (HHS), nursing babies compared with formula-fed babies have an enhanced immune response to polio, tetanus, diphtheria, and other viral infections. Nursing also increases the child's resistance to infectious diseases, such as diarrhea, respiratory tract infections, pneumonia, urinary infections, and others. Recent studies suggest that breastfeeding may also reduce the risk of type 1 and 2 diabetes, childhood cancer, and asthma. In addition, many researchers believe that breastfeeding also enhances the cognitive development of children compared to bottle-fed babies, according to (HHS.) "Breastfed children are actually smarter than bottle fed children," says Lise Eliot.[15] They have about a five-point higher IQ than bottle-fed infants, according to Anderson.[16] There is so much scientific evidence that breastfeeding is beneficial for infants' general development, that the American Academy of Pediatrics (AAP) now recommends that "breastfeeding continue for at least 12 months, and thereafter for as long as mother and baby desire. The World Health Organization recommends continued breastfeeding up to 2 years of age or beyond."[17]

On top of all these benefits for the baby, breastfeeding turns out to be beneficial also for the mother: "Breastfeeding has several positive hormonal, physical, and psychological effects on the mother," according to the HHS's *Blueprint for Action on Breastfeeding.* It increases the levels of oxytocin; a hormone that stimulates uterine contraction, minimizes postpartum maternal blood loss, and may reduce the risk of premenopausal and possibly postmenopausal breast cancer. The risk of ovarian cancer may also be lower among women who have breastfed their children. In addition, breastfeeding may have positive psychological effects on the mother, such as boosting her self-confidence, and strengthening the bond between mother and baby.

According to William Sears, a Canadian pediatrician and author, breastfeeding mothers respond to their babies more intuitively than bottle-fed babies. "I have noticed that breastfeeding mothers tend to show a high degree of sensitivity to their babies, and I believe this is a result of the biological changes that occur in a mother in response to the signals of her baby."[18]

Not less important is the fact that breastfeeding is more convenient; clean and always readily available compared with a bottle of formula. It is also more economic. "Families can save several hundred dollars over the cost of feeding breast milk substitutes," according to the Department of Health and Human Services.

I could not summarize the benefits of breastfeeding better than Gale Pryor, a science writer and author, in the following excerpt from *Nursing Mother, Working Mother: The Essential Guide for Breastfeeding and Staying Close to Your Baby after You Return to Work*:

> As scientists have amply documented, breast milk benefits every system in a baby's body. Breastfeeding offers protection against allergies and respiratory infections, and perhaps obesity. Breastfeeding improves vision and oral development; breastfed babies have fewer ear infections; breast milk is better for the cardiovascular system and kidneys; and babies' intestinal immunity is enhanced by human milk, Juvenile diabetes is less common among breastfed than bottle-fed babies. Breastfeeding enhances a baby's cognitive development, partially because it allows the baby more control in feeding. The composition of breast milk, too, appears to support optimal brain development. . . studies have found that children fed mother's milk as babies have higher IQ, on average, than those fed formula.[19]

As for the baby's emotional development, Pryor continues:

> A baby's emotional need for love and reassurance is just as strong as her physical need for milk. Whereas most

formula-fed babies are soon taught to hold their own bottle, the breastfed baby is always held by her mother for feedings. A breastfed baby thus enjoys not only the comfort of the warm breast, but also the caressing, rocking, and eye contact with mother before, during, and after feedings.[20]

According to the American Academy of Pediatrics, breast milk alone is sufficient to support a baby's optimal growth and development for approximately the first six months of life. By that time, other foods are slowly introduced, with breast milk remaining the main source of nutrients throughout the first year. Once the nursing period ends, well-balanced baby food and small portions from the parents' food should be provided; sensitively fitting the child's chewing ability and digestive development.

Beyond Feeding, Diapers, and a Bath

Next in importance to nutrition is keeping the infant warm and clean. Fresh diapers must be provided as often as needed, with other clean clothing items fitting the seasonal requirements. Daily warm baths are recommended, with light massages, to prevent diaper rash, and to soothe and relax the child's muscles and nerves. The sense of touch is among a baby's most advanced abilities at birth. Touch is essential to sensory-motor development. According to Lise Eliot, the neuroscientist at Chicago Medical School, there is evidence that children who are treated to daily massages by their parents show lower anxiety and stress levels, along with better mood, improved sleep patterns, and higher levels of attention,. Exposure to fresh air, weather permitting, and a little sun is also recommended, to help develop and strengthen the child's lungs, respiratory system, and bones.

Attention must be given also to the baby's physical environment. The child should be kept in a safe, clean, and quiet place—be it a crib, a playpen in the corner of a room, or in the child's nursery—keeping in mind the infant's need, during the first year, for extensive periods of sleep also during the day. A hanging mobile, crib guards with a vivid pattern, a picture on the wall, a few stuffed animals, picture books, and some baby toys are also important to slowly help stimulate the child's sensory systems, language development, and growing mind (more on this point later).

Sensitivity to the noise level around the house is also important. As mentioned earlier, babies can hear before they are born. Most fetuses begin hearing early in the sixth month of gestation. Exposure to high levels of noise can be irritating within the womb as well as after the child is born. Keep in mind, however, that infants and youngsters of all ages love music. They find music enjoyable from the moment they are born. They find soft quiet music to be soothing and relaxing, while loud metallic sounds can be irritating and unnerving. This is why youngsters of all cultures love lullabies, which are usually soft, quiet, and calming. Parents can play this type of music for their children from early on to calm and relax them.

While a baby's motor development is genetically programmed, and all babies develop through the same sequence, experience does play an important role in a child's motor development. So baby-proof your home, and give your child freedom to move and stretch his limbs. The child's muscles and bones need to be used in order to properly develop. And the more the child will stretch and move her muscles and bones, the better they will develop. Provide also plenty of experiences to gently stimulate all the child's senses—auditory, visual, and also smell, touch, and taste (without overdoing). Remember that it's through sensory input that the brain is stimulated to develop, as will be addressed in the following section.

Parents are responsible for the child's health, dispensing all needed medications, including taking the child to the pediatrician's office for regular checkups and inoculations. Mothers usually shoulder this responsibility, unless they entrusts this function to another responsible adult. It is always good to keep in mind Brazelton and Greenspan's words of advice that too many children are exposed to unnecessary risks and are born with low birth weight and with preventable physical, learning, emotional, and social difficulties. Early abuse and neglect also make many babies vulnerable to alterations in their central nervous system, the two experts warn. And prenatal and postnatal exposure to alcohol, tobacco, lead, mercury, and other toxic substances are another risk factor undermining healthy central nervous system functioning.

Once a baby's basic physical needs are satisfied, chances are good that the child will grow adequately in length and weight, and acquire the developmental touch points (to use Brazelton's signature term) of looking, listening, holding up its head; rolling from stomach to back and from back to stomach; then sitting up, crawling, standing, and so forth.

Parents-to-be often assume that these are in a nutshell the essentials of childcare during the first year of life—namely, feeding, changing diapers, giving a bath, rocking a crying baby to sleep, doing some hugging and cooing, with an occasional visit to the doctor's office for checkups and inoculations. Many think that all a baby does is eat, sleep, and cry. And since it is programmed from birth, the baby will in due time begin to naturally sit, stand, walk, and talk, following its genetic blueprint. But while it may have been the common understanding in the past, this is no longer the case today.

With our new tools to look inside the brain, we now have a better understanding of how the brain works. With the greater insight gained in the last few decades into child development, we can now observe how the environment affects the brain's workings. Our understanding of what takes place in those early years of life has changed. We now know there is much more to proper childcare and good mothering during the early years than was previously thought, and much more to healthy child development. We now know about the importance of early experience, and the existence of critical periods of development. We know what can stimulate brain cells to grow and develop, and that pruning of unused neurons (brain cells) occurs.

This information is important for parents and anyone else who is involved with childcare. This knowledge can make the difference between raising a bright and highly developed child or a dull slow-developing one. But I am getting ahead of myself, so let me pause for some clarification.

Early Brain Development

The human brain is built out of billions of brain cells, or neurons, each of which is shaped like a tree. As Lise Eliot, the neuroscientist explains, "A mature neuron has an extensive root system, called the dendrites, that receives input from other neurons, and a trunk, or axon, that can be extremely long and ultimately branches out to relay information to the next neurons in the circuit."[21] This information is transmitted electrically from one axon to another and the point of contact between axons is called a synapse. The human brain has some 100 billion neurons most of which are present by the midpoint of gestation. But this is just the beginning of brain development. With just a tiny axon at first, a few short dendritic branches, and virtually no synaptic connections, these neurons cannot do a thing. The real business of brain development is in synaptic formation (synaptogenesis), the bulk of which begins through gestation and continues through much of the first year, and in some regions well into the second year of life.

"Synaptogenesis occurs at a rate of 1.8 million new synapses per second between two months of gestation and two years after birth," says Eliot.[22] But in order to accommodate this massive synaptic formation the neurons have to expand their dendritic branching. And this involves an "intricate dance between nature and nurture." In other words, it is experience that pushes dendritic and synaptic formation, thus in effect sculpturing the brain. It is important to remember that synapses that are highly active get stabilized. Synapses that are less activated atrophy and are pruned away. Stimulating environment will stimulate abundant brain growth. We have the technology today to compare images of brains that have been stimulated by rich activities and experience with images of brains that developed in a non-stimulating environment, and see the difference. The stimulated brains are much thicker and bigger than the non-stimulated brains, because of the more complex and abundant circuitry of dendrites and synapses.

As Eliot puts it: "A young child's environment directly and permanently influences the structure and eventual function of his or her brain. Everything a child sees, touches, hears, feels, tastes, thinks and so on, translates into electrical activity."[23] This activity leaves its mark on the wiring of the child's brain—growing a new dendrite, forming a new synapse, or strengthening a point of contact that has been established before. There are periods in which the brain is more ready and receptive to master certain new skills, as for example, learning to talk, recognizing the alphabet, or mastering a second language. These are considered "critical" or "sensitive" periods. Once a given brain region has "passed the refinement stage," its critical period has ended, it will no longer be as open and ready to learn that skill, and opportunity to rewire it is significantly reduced.

Imagine the great opportunity that parents have to actually shape the complexity, density, and potential function of their child's brain. Irrespective of the brain's genetic makeup at birth, it is the child's experience after birth that counts for so much more; especially during the first two to three years of life when the brain circuitry is being established. Once that early sensitive period has passed, the basic infrastructure of the child's brain will be established. Any later information the child will acquire will be filed in the drawers of the foundational infrastructure that you, the parents, helped to establish. Or, to make another analogy, it will be added on to the original tapes. This is why the quality of this basic infrastructure is so important. This is why it is so critical to surround young children with a stimulating environment (carefully avoiding overstimulation). The manner in which you raise your child during these few early years will greatly determine if it will be bright or dull, much more than his or her genetic make-up. This is true irrespective of your social or economic conditions. It is that simple.

Social/Emotional Development

Emotions dominate our early life more than they will ever again. Before they master language babies communicate through crying, smiling, fussing, and cooing. Through these emotional expressions and the responses they get to these, babies develop their feelings of security and confidence, their disposition, and the motivation to strive and master the difficult motor, verbal, and cognitive challenges ahead of them.

"Nurturing emotional relationships are the most crucial primary foundation for both intellectual and social growth,"[24] say Brazelton and Greenspan, the renowned child development experts, in *The Irreducible Needs of Children*:

> The most dramatic recent example of the results of neglecting a small child's needs are the orphanages in Romania and other countries that were doing little more than warehousing infants and young children. In these settings, without warm nurturing or appropriate social and intellectual interactions, children developed severe physical, intellectual, and social deficits. Four- or five-year-olds were able to communicate only with a few simple gestures, such as reaching for food. When upset, these children would often frantically bang or sometimes bite their own arms. They had no language or ability to use pictures to communicate basic needs or wants, let alone more rapid communications, and only fleeting capacities to receive comfort or warmth when hurt or upset.[25]

What makes these stories even more distressing is that when these children are later adopted, to good home environments, it is often difficult to remedy their condition. Once the critical period of the early years has passed, their brain wiring has been established, and it becomes difficult to rewire and change its functional pattern.

So of all the foundational feelings that a young child must experience love is the most important. As Ann Dally, the British psychiatrist puts it: "Of all that the child absorbs from the good mother . . . the most important are probably loving feelings that are not contingent. . . . The important thing is that basically she is on his side and, no matter what he does or how he develops, she remains that way."[26] Let us take a closer look.

The Effect of a Mother's Love

Why is it so important to feel loved from the beginning of infancy? Why would it matter to a baby who hardly understands anything, or for that matter a well- fed toddler, whether he or she is loved—to the point of occasionally giving up altogether and dying if that need for love is not satisfied? What does a baby know about love?

Love and Survival

It is interesting that the need for love is universal. Babies all over the world demonstrate this need through their strong attachment to their mother. In fact, the newborns of all mammals display a need for intense mothering; a period of ongoing nurturing relationship with their mother, whose proximity they seek, and who becomes their primary attachment figure—their base of security. Irrespective of whether it is a human baby, a monkey infant, a puppy, a fawn, or a rat pup, they all need and seek, in addition to food and shelter, the warmth, protection, licking, fondling, modeling, nudging, the sense of belonging, and later, guidance, of their mother. It appears that without these basic ingredients, mammals, including humans, cannot thrive, and occasionally will even die.

Feelings of attachment appear to be rooted in our genetic makeup. It is "programmed into limbic development," says Lise Eliot, to ensure the parental care on which survival depends. "Attachment behaviors are prominent in every species of bird or mammal whose survival depends heavily on parental care," adds Eliot.[27] That is the reason why breastfeeding, which facilitates the bonding between mother and infant, is so powerful. And the process of attachment—which probably begins with milk when nursing gets under way—develops through the nervous system and the sense of touch, as part of the feeding and socialization process. The sense of touch as we know it is considered to be of primary importance from the beginning of life, no less important than the auditory and visual senses.

Moreover, helpless and weak at birth, and dependent on their mother, infants survive because of an inherent maternal desire to take care of them and nurture them. The maternal desire to take care of a baby is also programmed into the genetic make-up of mothers and is possibly activated by a woman's hormones once she gives birth to a child. Thus we see that the mother/infant bond is not only a social convention, but also a biologically driven emotion that is fueled by a surge of hormones from two directions—the mother's and the baby's. Since the nursing process affects the hormonal state of a mother (increasing the levels of oxytocin, for example), nursing mothers may feel a stronger attachment to their infants (see Dr. William Sears's statement on that point).

A Mother's Love Encourages Child's Empathy

Attachment behavior is important not only for an infant's physical survival. Studies found that family patterns that undermine nurturing care may lead to significant compromise in both cognitive and emotional capacities. Supportive, warm, nurturing emotional interactions with infants and young children help the central nervous system to grow appropriately, say Brazelton and Greenspan. When there are secure, empathetic nurturing relationships, children learn to be intimate and empathetic and eventually to communicate about their feelings, reflect on their own wishes, and develop their own relationships with peers and adults.

New information from brain research indicates that children's ability to deal with moral issues and perceive higher-level emotions such as love develops around the ages of one to three. This capacity, according to Ray Kurzweil, a world-renowned scientist and best-selling author, is handled by special neural cells called spindle cells, which are found only in humans and some great apes.[28] These special cells do not exist in newborn humans but begin to appear only at around the age of four months and increasing significantly from ages one to three. Now MRI scans reveal that spindle cells are activated in situations that deal with high level emotions such as love, anger, or sadness. This is an important finding which may explain why children raised in orphanages, where their emotions are neglected or ignored, have so many developmental and relations difficulties. This finding provides another confirmation for the critical importance of the preschool years for children's development.

Children's thinking ability is also affected when they are surrounded by empathetic relationships and when they feel secure. They become relaxed, and once they are relaxed their thinking becomes clear. "Emotions are actually the internal architects, conductors, or organizers of our minds. They tell us how and what to think, what to say and when to say it, and what to do. We 'know' things through our emotional interactions and then apply that knowledge to the cognitive world," argue Brazelton and Greenspan.[29]

A Mother's Love and Character Development

Character and personality development are also affected by a mother's love. Babies have no sense of self. Driven at first by a bundle of instincts, they begin to imitate their parents. Even newborns can imitate different facial expressions. Some infants will mimic both parents, but more often they mimic the parent who is the primary attachment figure—the parent who spends the greater amount of time with the child, caring for and nurturing it. The child will feel closest to that parent and try to emulate her or him. The stronger the bond between parent and child, the stronger will be the child's sense of identity and belonging, emulating personal characteristics of that parent and blending them with the child's own inherent temperamental features. A strong parent-child bond in the early years will carry into later years, if the parents so desire and keep working at it. And the stronger that bond the stronger will be the child later in life to stand against an adverse environment such as negative peer pressure, for example.

Children's moral sense, the ability to distinguish between right and wrong, is also rooted in early emotional interactions between parent and child; The ability to understand another person's feelings and to care about how he or she feels can arise only from experience with a nurturing environment. We can feel empathy only if someone has been empathetic and caring for us. We cannot experience emotions that were never shown to us. If parents are cold to their children, ignoring their valid feelings, or expecting them to suppress these, those children will likely grow to become cold to others, ignoring their feelings and pain.

Although it is true that infants can establish relationships with more than a single individual, they prefer their mother. As Eliot explains, "Whoever is the most consistent caregiver, the one who most reliably fulfills a baby's physical and emotional needs, will become his or her primary attachment figure. Mothers tend to have the advantage here, especially if they're nursing," says Elliot.[30]

In conclusion, it is immaterial what is stronger, a baby's need to feel loved and attached, or a mother's feelings of attachment toward her baby. It is an instinctive dance for life in which mother and child are the partners. This dance will leave its mark on the rest of the child's life. And its tune will color all future interactions, either warming the heart or chilling it, depending on the quality of that first dance.

Children's Mental Development

Infants are born with a sensitive, growing brain—a brain that will increasingly take control of the child's physical and social/emotional functions, as well as mental activity. As mentioned earlier, the brain's potential in the early years of life develops faster than at any other period—eagerly activating its dormant neurons, stretching out dendrites, and forming synapses to connect different neurons. This early brain activity lays the foundation, the infrastructure so to speak, for the child's lifelong physical-social-emotional and mental function.

The child's environment, and the adults who are in charge of that environment, have, therefore, immeasurable opportunity to affect the developing brain's potential and to shape its future mental capability. As Greenspan puts it: "From the very beginning of life, there is thus a robust interaction between nature and nurture. Indeed, we might even say that optimal mental growth *requires* cooperation between them."[31] Greenspan then continues: "There is mounting evidence that environmental influences can alter the physical structure of the brain, determining in part how genes express themselves in both biology and behavior. Even when a genetic influence has been well established, subtle environmental factors may still operate."[32] Let us take the development of memory as an example.

Memory

One's ability to recall objects, memorize words, remember people and events, or understand concepts, and so on, is fundamental to learning. It is essential to many aspects of cognitive growth. Babies begin life with a primitive set of memory skills that start growing and develop. As mentioned earlier in this chapter, certain maternal nutritional supplements during pregnancy appear to improve an offspring's memory. But while memory skills at birth vary from one individual to another, some are born with a faster and more efficient way of coding and retrieving information than others. Studies indicate that only 40 percent of the variation in memorizing ability is attributed to genes, according to Eliot. Most of one's memory skills are determined by something other than genes. The common assumption is that this is experience. "Like any other skill, memory improves with practice—with repeated, deliberate effort to acquire and hold on to new information," notes Eliot.[33]

The early years are critical for the development of memory because the basic circuitry underlying conscious memory storage is being laid down during these years. The more parents activate that circuitry, the more it will develop. "The more a child is challenged to use her memory, even early on, the better it is likely to serve her later in life," says Eliot.[34] Your child's ability to memorize words, events, concepts, people, names, and the like, will affect his or her general learning ability throughout life. This capability is in your hands to develop. You can sharpen your child's learning capacity or dull it, depending on the type and amount of experiences you will provide for him or her.

How can one sharpen a child's memory, you'll ask? Keep asking from an early age, many questions of who, what, when, where, how, and why. Sing aloud favorite songs together with your child repeatedly. Read aloud to your child favorite stories over and over again, discussing the content of the stories and the events they describe. What parent does not want to have a bright child? So try to sharpen your child's memory skills. Think about that as you drive along with your toddler, or as you walk the supermarket aisles grocery shopping with him or her. A few minutes here, a few minutes there, of attentive questions or quizzes about common repeated labels, can improve your child's memory skills for life.

Language

If parents spend the first year of their child's life worrying about physical development, they devote the second year to language. They eagerly await every new word and utterance or nervously look for language charts, reading up about language delays and disorders. The good news is that the vast majority of children learn their language with no problem. The brain is hardwired for language. "Language has its own neural apparatus," says Eliot. But while the capacity for language may be encoded in the genes, a child's mastery of language depends on his or her experience.

Early language immersion is necessary for language ability to develop. This is true for all children in all languages worldwide. Children who are not exposed to language communication from an early age may end up permanently incapable of learning and using language. The literature is replete with such examples. So language, like vision and most other brain functions, is bounded by a critical period, an early phase in which a child must experience language, or else its special hardware won't wire up right, writes Eliot.[35]

The quality of language that children experience during these early critical years varies from one child to another. But we now know that children who have a rich language experience at home—from an early age—acquire a much better language facility than children who come from homes with poor or little verbal communication. It is hard to close that gap in later school years.

One may wonder why a newer, immature brain is so much better at learning grammar and mastering pronunciation than an older, more mature one. The answer lies in the plasticity, of the young newer system. Early in life, when the number of synapses in the child's brain is at its peak, and before the division between the left and the right brain hemispheres sets in, presents the greater opportunity for selecting optimal neural pathways for language development.

This means that parents and other caregivers can affect children's language development. Studies indicate that several features make the greatest difference in determining this development. These features include: (1) the amount of parents' talking to their children—children whose parents addressed or responded to them more in early life had larger, faster-growing vocabularies, and scored higher on IQ tests than children whose parents spoke fewer words to them overall, and (2) the amount of positive versus negative feedback that children hear is also important. It appears that youngsters who hear a large proportion of *no, don't, stop it,* and so forth, have poorer language skills than three-year-olds who had received more positive feedback. Negative feedback may lower the confidence level of children, lessening their interest and attention span, and deflating their attempts to ask questions, engage in conversations, memorize new words, in short, develop their language.

Language stimulation should begin very early in life, ideally from birth. At first, the sounds of the language should be introduced—ba-ba-ba, ma-ma-ma, and so forth. Then (around three months) children can be engaged in labeling play in which parents start naming objects, people's names, and action, and then verbs. Around nine months of age, short sentences should be introduced. Special books on young children's language development are available in public libraries, bookstores, and on the Internet. Yet the most important feature for parents to remember is to talk, talk, and talk with their child, keeping in mind that the quantity of language exposure is critical. The more words a child hears, the larger his or her vocabulary will be. The words have to be addressed to the child, referring to something that he or she can relate to; only then can the child make sense of language. Furthermore, the language spoken with young children must be simple, clear, and positive, with lots and lots of repetitions. And lastly, don't forget to listen to the child, and not just do the talking—avoiding excessive corrections.

Since preschoolers love word games and making up rhymes, parents can be creative and invent word games with their children. They can do that throughout the day—while driving in the car with a youngster strapped in the car seat; while fixing dinner with a toddler playing on the floor at his mother's feet; or walking along the supermarket aisles selecting food items, and so forth. Be playful with your language communications with your child. There are no special rules to follow. The main point is to talk a lot with your child—using good, clear, and positive language—about any topic of interest, and to enjoy these communications.

Youngsters also love books and being read to. Plenty of books are available for every age group, providing another great source for language learning—enriching the child's vocabulary, listening skills, imagination, and, not less important, literacy development. The foundation for children's reading ability begins to develop naturally during these early preschool literacy experiences. The more you read to your child, the easier it is for him or her to acquire the necessary skills for reading. So carry on conversations with your child, about anything that is of interest to you or the child, keeping in mind that the critical period for language development is between birth and ages six or seven. It appears that some linguistic doors get closed around that age. Second language acquisition, for instance, which is relatively easily mastered by preschoolers, and with no accent, becomes quite difficult at a later age, and is always accompanied with a heavy accent. Although young children do continue to increase their vocabulary in later years (in fact throughout life), their linguistic development is then much slower. And it will always be based on the linguistic foundation that was established and encoded in their brain circuitry in the early formative years.

Intelligence

The Webster dictionary defines intelligence as the ability to learn or understand from experience; an ability to acquire or retain knowledge, or to respond successfully to a new situation. Intelligence has to do with wisdom—with being smart about life and how to manage it. The early years are important for the development of intelligence. Already years ago Benjamin Bloom, a noted educational psychologist, concluded that "from conception to age four, the individual develops 50% of his mature intelligence, from age four to eight he develops another 30%, and from ages eight to seventeen the remaining 20%."[36]

In fact, we now know that the brain of a newborn is one-quarter of its adult size (roughly half a pound). It will triple in size in the first year and be full grown (nearly three pounds) by the time a child is five years of age, according to Eliot. The cause for this rapid early growth is the fast synaptic and dendritic formation during the early years. We can now say that a child's cognitive development—his ability to retain and acquire information, to reason, to have a longer attention span, to better grasp concepts, and to better problem solve skills—is the product of two interacting influences: brain growth and experience. These two influences are most potent in the early years when synapses are forming at a fast rate, and the brain is in the height of its plasticity.

There is general agreement that both heredity and environment play a part in determining how smart a child will be; the debate is only over percentage: how much is nature, and how much is nurture. Opinions range all the way from strict "environmentalists," who believe that early rearing, education, and culture, mostly influence a child's intelligence, to "hereditarians," who believe that genes have the major influence. Behavioral geneticists concluded that it is about half and half, with genes accounting for about half of one's IQ score, leaving the other half to the environment, with early experience being critical for children's later intellectual potential. As Eliot puts it: "Brain wiring *needs* stimulation. Synapses wither and dendrites will fail to sprout without the steady buzz of neural activity that comes from new and varied experiences. Genes create the blueprint, but actually growing the neural networks inside each child's head requires a steady stream of vigorous interactions with other people, objects, places, and events in the world."[37]

And so we see how learning begins at birth, with parents being the children's first and most important teachers. It is not surprising that maternal teaching is also linked with school readiness. There is in fact a large body of literature indicating that parent–child interactions in the home are associated with school readiness. A recent article by Pia Britto, Jeanne Brooks-Gunn and Terri Griffin, for example, studying maternal teaching patterns among low-income African American families with low school achievements found that "verbal guidance and language use emerge as salient aspects of maternal interaction strongly linked with child outcomes. These results, as well as others, suggest that preschoolers whose mothers provided them with high levels of support and guided participation demonstrated greater school readiness and expressive language use when compared with children who received low levels of maternal engagement."[38]

Discipline

One cannot discuss the mother's role without addressing the issue of discipline— the teaching of proper behavior. Discipline, after all, has been a central aspect of child rearing from the beginning of human civilization, and parents in all cultures have had to deal with this issue. "Next to love, discipline is a parent's second most important gift to a child," says T. Berry Brazelton. No civilized society can function without a developed form of discipline among the majority of its people. Volumes have been written on the topic. And copies can be found on shelves of all major bookstores and libraries.

In this section I will touch on only a few points that are especially relevant to the early years of childhood, when the brain is the most ready to learn and patterns of behavior are newly set and formed. It is much easier to imprint on a child's brain good patterns of behavior early on rather than to correct bad patterns years later.

So here are a few important points to remember during the first few years of a child's life:

1. A sense for discipline needs to be developed from an early age, when a child starts to understand simple instructions. When eight months old babies, for example, pull on a mother's hair, or poke her face, with no intention to harm, she can divert the child's attention, or hold his hand and say, "I don't like it, it hurts, and I'll hold your hand until you stop doing that." After several such exchanges the baby will learn to stop that behavior.

    Twelve months old babies may run away from you, to test their limit. How do you discipline a twelve months old baby not to run from you on a busy street corner? You react firmly saying, "you cannot do this ever again." After several such attempts and their prompt restraint by you, the baby will learn to obey you.

    Eighteen months old youngsters may throw a temper tantrum or display violently negative behavior, when they try to develop a sense of independence, so how do you stop such behavior? You remain calm, never yelling back at the child, knowing that this is a natural phase of development. If possible leave the room, ignoring the child, thus displaying that such behavior does not impress you. Once the child is calm you can discuss with him or her why that behavior is inappropriate.

2. Children must understand from an early age that parents set the rules and the children are expected to obey them.

3. Parents need to be consistent in their instructions and their expectations, and watch for mixed messages.

4. Instructions to children need to be clear and firm, and parents need to see that these are followed. It is always important

to explain to a child why a particular instruction is given, or why it is important.

5. Discipline should be viewed as teaching and NOT as punishment. Physical discipline, such as hitting or spanking a child, is no longer accepted as a good form of discipline. "Instead of punishment, parents need to take every opportunity to sit down with a child and say 'Every time you do this, I must stop you, until you can stop yourself,'" counsel Brazelton and Greenspan.[39]

6. Reassure your child that you love him or her when disciplining, and do not be bossy.

7. Children thrive in a structured environment; It gives them a sense of security and peace. They may occasionally try to test their limits, but they will enjoy it overall.

8. Whenever discipline does not work, stop and reevaluate.

Summary Points

Most parents would like their children to be bright and successful in school and in life. There are certain things you can do to increase the probability of having healthy, bright, and well-behaved children:

1. Remember that 20 percent of a child's intelligence is determined by prenatal factors that influence fetal brain development, such as a mother's health, nutrition, environmental exposure, and emotional well-being. Therefore, pregnant women should be under medical supervision; have a healthy diet rich with vitamins, minerals, and trace elements; and get enough sleep, regular exercise, and keep their stress level down. It is also recommended that the mother abstain from alcohol and cigarettes, which are known to affect brain development.

2. Once a baby is born, the single most important nutritional choice a mother can make is to breastfeed. As mentioned earlier, children reared on breast milk are healthier than formula-fed babies and score some eight points higher on IQ tests at eight years of age compared to those reared on formula. The American Academy of Pediatrics recommends breastfeeding for a full year after birth. If breastfeeding is not possible, nutritional guidance by a pediatrician should be carefully followed.

3. Never forget that brain development requires stimulation. Smarter children come from homes that provide young children with ample opportunity to explore and a great variety of playthings. Children need also to get out of the home—for walks to the park, the library, the store, to other people's homes to see other children and their parents and how they interact with each other.

4. Children learn from a variety of activities in a stimulating environment. But more important than all these activities is the quality of interaction between a child and his or her parents. A number of parenting features are consistently related to kids' emotional, intellectual and academic success. These include:
    Being physically affectionate and emotionally supportive of the children
    Being involved with the children
    Being responsive to their needs
    Being a demanding parent; that is, expecting appropriate behavior, setting clear standards and rules, and seeing that these are followed.

5. Formal preschool education before age four is not necessary if parents can provide their children a stimulating environment that is rich with age-appropriate toys, materials, books, music, art, a variety of activities, and play experience with other children. However, attending a good half-day preschool, three times a week, at ages three to five, can provide enrichment for a child and some free time for the mother. Several different types of preschool education are available in the United States, each having a different curriculum and educational objectives; from play-oriented programs to academic programs. Different children could benefit from different types of programs. It is important to match the child with the right program for him or her. See *How to Choose a Nursery School* for details.[40]

The "Perfect" Parent

All together, there is obviously a lot that parents can do to improve their children's developmental prospects, so much so that some potential parents may get cold feet and choose to remain childless. For these parents-to-be I would like to quote an eloquent humorous page from Lise Eliot's book. I couldn't say it any better:

> The perfect parent, if she (or he) existed, would devote herself full time to the care and teaching of her child. She would begin, even before conception, by shoring up her folic acid reserves and purging her body of any chemical remotely suspect. Once pregnant, she would never touch a drop of alcohol, pump her own gasoline, get less than eight hours sleep, or allow herself to be stressed in any way. She would have an ideal, unmedicated, and uncomplicated delivery, and breastfeed from the moment of birth until the child was potty-trained.[41]

And Eliot continues:

She would know precisely how to stimulate her baby, but also how to avoid overstimulation. She would spend hours every day playing with him—singing, cuddling, talking, massaging, exercising, reading, showing him how all kinds of toys and other fascinating objects work—and never have to leave him in his swing for half an hour while trying to make supper or balance the checkbook. Her house would be perfectly baby-proofed, so he could explore every corner and rarely hear "No!" She'd take him on all kinds of different outings, always giving him her full attention, and never grow annoyed when he pulled all the vitamins off the shelf at the pharmacy or whined for cookies at the grocery store. She'd introduce him to other children, all with similarly perfect parents, and gladly clean up after the messiest play dates.[42]

And Eliot concludes:

She'd start him on piano/tennis/dance/French/swimming/ art/violin/computer/Spanish/tumbling lessons at age three (practicing herself, to provide a good role model) but, if he showed no interest, would happily forfeit the ten weeks' tuition. She'd send him to the perfect preschool, using their time apart to brush up on the latest child-rearing information and prepare all sorts of new and interesting educational activities for him. And of course, she wouldn't do it alone. She'd have the "perfect spouse" right alongside, equally loving/stimulating/nurturing/teaching their child every step of the way. . . .Parenting is hard, hard work. Most of us try the best we can, given the limits on our time, stamina, and resources. Of course, we'd all like to do more for our children, to be a little more perfect in the parenting department. I've yet to meet a mother or father who doesn't feel guilty at times, wishing she or he had more time, patience, or money to devote to each child. These are the moments when it's reassuring to remember the other half of the equation: heredity. Given that even the perfect parent doesn't have "perfect genes," maybe we can relax just a little bit and enjoy our kids for who they are. [43]

Conclusion

This chapter highlighted the importance of the first few years of life and the centrality of parents, in particular mothers, in shaping their children's development during this period. Many parents intuitively understand that. As de Marneffe put is: "caring for young children is something mothers often view as extraordinarily important both for their children and for themselves."[44] Yet too many other parents do not realize just how critically important they are during these first few years of life. Lacking this understanding they often make poor childcare decisions.

Can an extended use of daycare substitute for mother care with good outcome? This is a question that hasn't gone away since the 1970s. But after thirty years of observation and research, we finally have a definitive answer. Let us move to the next chapter for some concluding thoughts about daycare.

CHAPTER FIVE

DAYCARE'S ILLUSION

Many parents remain ignorant about how really bad the childcare is that their children are receiving.

–Sharon L. Ramey, *Child Care and Child development*

The Daycare Dilemma

Busy parents often ask how much time they need to spend with their infant or toddler; meaning, how much of their time young kids really need. They wonder whether quality time could substitute for quantity. According to T. Berry Brazelton, the renowned baby expert, most of a baby's waking time should be spent either in direct face-to-face interactions with caregivers or with a caregiver being in sight. "While awake, babies shouldn't be out of sight," he says.[1]

As the idea of daycare became increasingly attractive to working parents, seeming to conveniently solve their childcare needs, we saw the growing concern among mental health experts about the institutional care of preschool children and its long-term negative effect on their development. Stanley Greenspan, the renowned child psychiatrist of George Washington University and one of the most vocal opponents of daycare, has argued emphatically against the placement of infants and toddlers (during the first two years of life) in full-time, (30- to 40-plus-hour week) daycare. Most day-care centers do not provide high-quality care, says Greenspan, and the quality of interactions between caregivers and babies is often less than optimal. "The current ratios of four babies per caregiver in the first year and six in the second year, coupled with high staff turnover, minimum wages, insufficient training . . . make it difficult to provide high-quality, ongoing, nurturing care in those early years," he elaborates.[2]

Many potential parents do not think ahead carefully, says Greenspan. They want to have children and a good career, and they see no problem. What they're being led to believe now is that full-time day care in the first years of life is as good as if not better than what they can provide. "I'll have a baby, take a two month leave of absence, put the baby in day care, and I'll be a lawyer and my spouse will be a lawyer. We'll work until 8:00 at night. We'll pick up the baby, come home, and play for an hour."[3] This is an illusion. In families like this, says Greenspan, children are not getting their basic needs for nurturing. Many parents are in denial, receiving a lot of misinformation, and are told that it doesn't make a difference. "If parents-to-be knew more about this need for a continuous, close relationship, they might plan more realistically," he adds.

The Importance of Continuity

As discussed in earlier chapters, continuous affectionate relationships are essential for regulating children's behavior, feelings, moods, and intellectual development. Continuous relationships enable the smooth development of attachment and they foster a sense of belonging. Continuity provides the child with a desirable model to identify with and emulate. It offers a reliable source for learning, and a trusted guiding hand for discipline. Continuous relationship also provides an emotional anchor for the child, a solid root. The type of interactions that are necessary for a child can take place in full measure only with a loving caregiver who has lots of time to devote to the child. A busy day-care provider, with four babies or six or eight toddlers usually won't have the time for these long sequences of interactions, emphasize Brazelton and Greenspan.[4] The high turnover of personnel in daycare centers also undermines the possibility of developing secure and confidence-building relationships with the children.

Moreover, if a child is lucky to be enrolled in a good center, with warm stable personnel, spending there a large portion of the day, another problem may arise. That child's sense of identity and belonging may get confused. It is true that preschoolers can become attached to multiple caregivers, but they cannot develop a sense of belonging to many caregivers. They will become most attached and feel the greatest sense of belonging to that person with whom they spend the greatest amount of warm awake time.

So a child who spends more waking hours in daycare than at home with a parent may become more attached to the center and that special provider. I saw children who do not want to go home when a parent comes to pick them up, preferring to stay in the relaxed center environment; or children who approach a loving provider calling her "Mommy," because they are confused about who is really the important person in their life. I have also seen mothers who become jealous when their child displays much love to a daycare provider (or for that matter, to a nanny). Does he still love me? Does he love her more? Are common maternal feelings in the daycare environment.

Preschoolers thrive on continuous individual relationships in a warm, stimulating environment. Spending long days in a daycare center is not the optimal environment for their development. A few hours—two or three times a week—beginning around age three, in a good center or preschool, will offer social and intellectual enrichment for children. But a daylong stay in a children's center could not replace the special bonding, nurturing, teachings, and exclusive sense of belonging that only a good parent can provide.

Choice or Necessity

Yet, feminists Susan J. Douglas and Meredith W. Michaels, speaking for many parents and daycare advocates, insist that "for most mothers, work is an absolute necessity," and that "some reliable form of childcare is also an absolute necessity."[5] The two women blame "dumb men" in the government for making "stupid choices" about childcare, and for refusing to support it. They target in particular the conservative right wing and the news media for helping propagate and disseminate those "stupid" choices. So what is a parent to do?

Douglas and Michaels and other daycare advocates praise some European countries, in particular Sweden, for being more enlightened about childcare than America, and more sensitive to women's needs. They consider Sweden to have "the best childcare system in the world," calling for a similar system to be established in the United States. So what is so special about the Swedish system? Let us take a brief look.

The Swedish Model

According to the Swedish Information Service[6] and OECD report (Organization for Economic Co-Operation and Development)[7] of 2001, Swedish infants between ages 0 to 1 year are looked after by a parent (generally, the mother) who gets 360 days of paid parental leave at 80 percent of earnings and another 60 SEK (Swedish Krona) daily for up to 90 days. Older preschoolers are entitled to daylong childcare as long as both parents work or go to school. Most Swedish preschools are run by the municipalities, but because of long waiting lists there is a growing number of independent schools (about 25 percent), half of which are parent cooperatives; 16.7 percent of Swedish preschoolers attend these independent preschools, which are not free. Parents may pay between 2 percent and 20 percent of their income for childcare, depending on their income and municipality fees. A proposal is now before Parliament to have free preschool for all children from age 4 years.

The main difference between the Swedish system and the American early childhood care and education system is: (a) the paid parental leave that Sweden provides for the first year of a child's life, and (b) a higher number of Swedish mothers of young children appear to be working outside their home with a reliance on the service of daycare (in 1999, 81.5 percent of women aged 25 to 34 years participated in the labor force; 32.1 percent worked part-time). Daycare advocates consider these two main points of difference worth emulating. Daycare critics dread this possibility, because of its potential negative long-term effect on the children's development—negative on a personal as well as a national level. Let us consider.

One Size Does Not Fit All

Sweden is a small socialist country with a total population of only nine million compared with the 300 million in the United States. Even with this much smaller number, Sweden cannot provide enough openings in its municipally run childcare to accommodate all their children. The Swedish system has, therefore, long waiting lists, and there is a growing trend to establish independent preschools, which may have poorer supervision and lower-quality standards.

Furthermore, since quality childcare is very expensive, tax rates in Sweden are much higher than in the United States. And it is unlikely that the American taxpayer would be ready (even under a new administration) for a significant tax hike in order to subsidize the daycare system for millions of children, especially as there is no evidence that the billions of dollars that have already been poured into the American early childhood education system have improved children's readiness for school.

As Sharon L. Ramey, professor of child and family studies at Georgetown University, and director of the Georgetown University Center on Health and Education, who is involved in national policymaking, puts it: "A number of recent books and articles identify literally scores of independently funded public and private initiatives—at many billions of dollars—to help young children get ready for school and to improve the quality of child care. Yet there is little indication that things really have improved" according to Ramey.[8]

The OECD report mentioned above, states that Sweden has a long tradition in research on early childhood. But unlike the United States, Sweden has not yet undertaken an extended study to evaluate the long-term effect of its childcare policy on Swedish children. It is true that the system serves women's needs, but what about the children and their development; And the lingering effect of that system on Sweden's future population?

It is beyond the scope of this book to further analyze the contemporary Swedish way of life (the growing decline of marriage, the sharp decline in birthrate, the rise in the number of unwed mothers, the fact that Sweden is the only country with more first birthing within cohabiting unions than marital unions,[9] and the declining productivity and overall Swedish economy—all of which are at much higher rates than in the United States). Sweden's population is also much more homogenous than the American population, having only one dominant culture, a fact that simplifies many educational issues, compared to the United States. But the core of the childcare issue, its very essence, is the question of what type of human beings we Americans want to raise.

Which system produces the healthier, more content, and more productive people? If the preschool years are a critical period for human development, and the bond between mother and young child is biologically encoded (remember, it is so for all mammals), then one must ask what is the cost for severing this bond too early, when the child is not yet ready for that.

The American Investigation of Daycare

Fortunately, we have now wonderful new sources of information that can help us clarify the daycare dilemma—and that is the recent findings from research. A large-scale American study is providing clear answers about the effect of daycare on participating children. The National Institute of Child Health and Human Development (NICHD) must be commended for taking the initiative and responsibility to embark on this massive study.

Alarmed by the growing rates of employment among married women with children under age 6 (including mothers of infants under age 2), and disappointed by the long list of studies that had produced conflicting results, the NICHD began in 1987 a large-scale longitudinal study to finally find out the truth about how early childcare arrangements affect children's development. The goal was to have "a study that would overcome many of the shortcomings of earlier research," and provide an authoritative guiding voice to help parents, early childhood professionals, politicians, and policymakers, who wondered how safe it is to place infants and toddlers in non maternal care.

The study had 3 phases, running from 1991-2004, and involving a large team of investigators from across the nation, collecting information on many variables related to child, family, and childcare characteristics. More than 1,300 children from diverse families in ten areas in the United States were followed from birth through age 3.

Children were assessed in terms of their physical growth and health, their social and emotional adjustment and family relations, infant-mother attachment, and cognitive and linguistic school readiness. Childcare environments and their effect were evaluated as well as the children's family and home environment. The study has produced over a hundred scientific publications by affiliated investigators, with many more still in press. The most important of these publications, covering the first 4.5 years of the children's lives, were compiled and published in 2005 in a volume titled *Child Care and Child Development*[10]. Future volumes are expected once later data are analyzed.

Examining the 400- plus pages of this first volume, one can only be impressed by the scope of the study and its quality. It is a wonderful addition to the research literature on early childhood care and development and a must-read resource for early childhood care and development specialists. But the findings of the study are a huge disappointment for daycare advocates. As Sharon L. Ramey who wrote the Commentary to the 2005 volume concluded, "these findings are an affirmation of what wise grandparents could have told us, and much more." An extensive use of daycare is not a good environment for young children's development.[11] So let us look at some of these findings.

Disappointing Findings

1. In terms of children's health, the NICHD study found that children in childcare get sick more often than children who are reared at home, experiencing more bouts of colds, coughs, ear infections, diarrhea, flu, and rashes. "Contemporary rates of communicable diseases are greater among children enrolled in child care during the first 2 years of life than among those who are not, the difference lessening at 3 years but increasing again between 3 and 4.5 years."[12]

2. As to the effect of daycare on   infants, the study found that infants who began non-parental care before their first birthday experienced many changes in their care arrangements, for a large number of reasons, and these changes had a negative effect on the children: "Children with more child care changes are more frequently classified as insecurely attached, are less competent with peers as toddlers, are more withdrawn and aggressive in preschool, and have more problems in school as first graders."[13] Moreover, any informal care arrangement at a child's home—by the father, grandparents, and in-home sitters whether part-time or full-time—was found to be better than a childcare center or childcare home.[14]

3. In terms of the intellectual development of children, the NICHD study indicates that participation in a good childcare program can have some benefit for children's intellectual development, especially if they come from homes that do not provide enough stimulation. But this advantage was found only for children who attended childcare centers, not childcare homes. Children in childcare homes or with babysitters did about the same intellectually as children at home with their mothers. And children who have a good stimulating home environment do not do any better, intellectually, when they have experience with daycare.

4. As for the social-emotional development of children, the study indicates that children who have experience with daycare centers demonstrate some advantage in social competence. But on the other hand, some studies also show that "children in childcare tend to be less polite, less agreeable, less compliant with their mothers' or caregivers' demands and requests, less respectful of others' rights, more irritable and rebellious, more likely to use profane language, more likely to be loud and boisterous, and more competitive and aggressive with their peers than children who are not or who have not been in day care."[15] These differences in aggressive and noncompliant behavior appear in tests as well as in natural observations, in childcare center and on the playground, with adults and with other children, with strangers and with parents, for children from both model and mediocre childcare programs,"[16] according to Clarke-Stewart and Allhusen.

    The NICHD study also found that the amount of time a child spends in daycare does matter. "The more time children spend in any of a variety of non-maternal care arrangements across the first 4.5 years of life, the more externalizing problems and conflict with adults they manifest at 54 months of age and in kindergarten."[17]

5. As to daycare's effect on the relationship between a mother and her child—one of the most sensitive issues in this study— "The findings show that extensive child care is associated with lower levels of maternal sensitivity."[18] The more time spent in childcare, for children ranging from six months to three years, was found to correlate with a lesser degree of maternal sensitivity. Daycare advocates are especially irate about this finding because low maternal sensitivity or responsiveness is

associated with a less secure attachment and poorer linguistic and cognitive development.

6. Another important finding of the NICHD study is its affirmation of the importance of the family and the home environment. Family, parents, and parenting skills do matter, the study concluded. "Children who received higher quality parenting as indicated by more sensitive, stimulating, and supportive maternal behavior at home and in semi-structured play displayed higher pre-academic skills, better language skills, more social skills, and fewer behavior problems than did children who received lower-quality parenting."[19]

A Conspiracy of Silence

In brief, the findings of the NICHD study are clearly negative, giving a straightforward response to parents who seek honest objective information about daycare. These findings are a huge disappointment to daycare advocates. And as Ramey observes, many people do not like hearing about them. This leads to a conspiracy of silence among scientists and professionals. "We dare not inflict even more guilt upon parents, or ask that they consider forgoing much needed outside income or spending more of their limited economic resources to obtain better quality care," says Ramey.[20]

Nonetheless, Ramey challenges the scientific and academic community to place children at the center of the agenda, and be honest when reporting about center-based childcare. When "People and groups are frankly fearful that criticism of existing standards and the quality of publicly funded programs ... will lead to a total withdrawal of any public support for very low-income families or those with two working parents ... many parents remain ignorant about how really bad the child care is that their children are receiving," she says.[21] This conspiracy of silence must be broken if we want to improve young children's environment and their early development. And this is the purpose of this chapter. But before we end it let us take a brief look at daycare in one other country.

Daycare in Britain

Also the British government has recently conducted an investigation of its daylong nurseries. And it appears that Britain has similar issues with daycare as the United States. Richard Garner, education editor of *The Independent Online Edition,* reports that parents in the UK spend less time with their children than parents in any other European country, because in growing numbers of British homes both parents go out to work. This leads to a "greater institutionalization" of children, writes Garner, quoting a teacher from Leeds who declared at a Teachers and Lecturers conference in Bornemouth, that "It does worry me that infants of only a few months are being cared for in a nursery environment for 10 hours a day, five days a week and 48 weeks a year."[22]

According to Garner's report, government research revealed that "children in full-time nursery settings were more likely to be antisocial, worried and upset" as compared with children who spent more time at home. The researchers noticed that "these children were more prone to tease other children, be bossy or stamp their feet." Yet, under public pressure, the British government has now embarked on a L370m drive to improve childcare and nursery facilities for children under five. And government ministers have pledged to a demanding public that there will be a nursery place for every three- and four-year-old child whose parents want them to be enrolled in a nursery program. Still, concerns are growing about the "institutionalization" of children, and the findings that indicate young people in the UK are more aggressive than young people in other European countries because they spend more time in under-five institutions. Overall, the British findings appear to support the American findings of the NICHD study.

Only 10 Percent of Mothers Want to Work Full-Time

Although the NICHD study is highly respected and definitive, it will take time for its findings to get disseminated and accepted by a public that has been bombarded for over three decades by a heavy pro daycare advocacy. The scientific and academic community is not alone in its silence about the daycare situation. Journalists also carry part of the blame. As Kate O'Beirne, the Washington editor of *National* Review puts it, "Feminist intimidation has created plenty of cowards." And she criticizes journalistic colleagues for being reluctant to publicly voice their concerns about childcare for fear that they'll be seen as advocating the return of women to the home full-time:[23]

"The feminist movement has long been on a collision course with what we know to be true about the natural bond between mother and child. . . . Women fall madly in love with their babies in a way that devoted fathers don't," writes O'Beirne.[24] And she happily reports the finding of a 2005 survey of working mothers which found that only 10 percent would choose to work full-time, while 30 percent would prefer to remain at home, and 59 percent would like part-time work[25] The majority of families with young children choose to get by on only one full-time salary, says O'Beirne.[26]

A similar population report by the U.S. Department of Commerce[27] also discloses that working mothers of preschool children prefer to leave their kids in the care of a relative rather than a non-relative. Only 12.7 percent of children in 2002 were cared for in daycare centers, and 6.2 percent in family daycare. While 12.7 percent is not an insignificant number, it is much smaller than what one would expect given the heavy publicity that daycare has received over the years.

Young children are totally dependant on their parents. Their welfare, and to a large extent their future, are in the parents hands. Conclusive information is now available about the negative effect of long hours spent in daycare. One can only hope that this information will reach the general public and parents will use it judiciously. It is true that American economy is now going through a difficult period, and many families experience financial hardship that may push more women to go out to work. But this is a temporary situation. America is a strong entrepreneurial nation. The current recession, like others before, will come to an end, and American economy will once again stabilize and rebound.

"American women have more freedom in their personal and professional lives than any man or woman has ever enjoyed in recorded history. The unprecedented opportunities we enjoy come with tough choices and trade-offs. Millions of women have learned they can have it all—fulfilling careers and families—but not at the same time unless they are willing to feel torn and conflicted. Many others make a different trade-off and try to sequence education, work, and children," writes Kate O'Beirne. [28]

Remember also that at issue are only a few years out of a woman's fifty to sixty years of adult life that should ideally be devoted to child rearing. Once a child goes to kindergarten a mother has much greater flexibility to pursue her own interests and needs without compromising her child's development.

The average twenty-first century man will change careers several times during his life span. I propose that the average twenty-first century woman consider dedicating ten years of her early adult life to intense mothering, a period in which she will give birth to two or three children, committing herself to stimulate their early development. Chapter 7 spells out this point.

CHAPTER SIX

SHOULD EVERY WOMAN BECOME A MOTHER?

Becoming a mother is absolutely the most demanding experience you can have in life, but it is also one of the most exhilarating and profound.

—*Alexandra Stoddard*, Mother

The Choice

"It should be a twenty-first century truism that not every woman needs to be a mother," states Inda Schaenen, a writer and teacher in a public-school system.[1] Both Schaenen's and Stoddard's, a prolific author herself, views are common in America today. So what is a woman to do? Should every woman try to become a mother? This is a new contemporary question. Up until a few years ago few would have raised this question, considering bearing and raising children to be a woman's main function. As Ann Dally, the perceptive British psychiatrist put it: "Until recently nearly every woman wished to be a mother and most women became mothers. To most it was automatic, part of being grown up and doing what was expected in the world."[2]

Moreover, until the mid-twentieth century there was systematic order in women's lives. Once they reached adulthood, women married, then started having babies (often lots of them), raised their family, managed their household, participated in community affairs, and sometimes worked outside their home, part-time or if necessary, full-time. While exceptions existed, this was the norm.

But as we saw in earlier chapters, things began to change during the twentieth century. Because of the radical developments that occurred since the 1960s there is no longer a single, invariable order in women's lives. Many lifestyles are now available. Many options are open, and many paths are possible. Contemporary American society allows every woman to choose whether to have children or not, when and how many children to have, and under what conditions to raise them—within marriage or out of marriage, together with a father, with two mothers, or alone; providing (mostly) maternal care in the early years of life, or primarily surrogate care, and so on and on. Children, who were considered essential and desirable in the not-so-distant past, are today a matter of personal choice, often complicating immeasurably a woman's life.

And yet, while there is great freedom to choose among the many alternatives, there is little direction or guidance about how to choose wisely. This results in a state of confusion. Women have difficulty choosing between becoming a mother or enjoying a carefree adventurous life; between first establishing a career and then becoming a mother, or first becoming a mother and then pursuing a career; between finishing one's education before having babies or finish it later on; between having children out of wedlock or not; between giving the child a father or raising a child without a father; and so forth. This is a dizzying array of choices, all within a woman's reach. So how does a woman decide which course to take? This chapter will explore relevant issues, to help a woman decide whether to have children or not and when is the best time to have them.

Most Women Love Children

To begin answer this question, it is important to first recognize that most women have an intrinsic love for children. This love is probably genetically encoded to ensure the survival of the species. The psychologist Daphne de Marneffe, for example, argues that her many interviews with women reveal that irrespective of the many options available to them today, women continue to hold on to the instinctive desire to have children; if not right away, at the beginning of their adult life, then somewhat later.

She observed in her clinical work, that this desire manifests especially when women face infertility problems. The repeated message one hears in these cases, says de Marneffe, even from the most committed professional women, is that "motherhood is all I really want from life." "When a woman contends with infertility, the desire to have a baby can become clear and keen and depthless; ambivalence about motherhood recedes until it is some distant and barely recognizable part of oneself. A vortex of yearning opens up at one's feet that suddenly, plainly, has been there forever. . . . Wanting a baby becomes the truest thing one has ever known about oneself," says de Marneffe.[3] Not less important is her observation that most women, also long to nurture and raise their babies and young children.

The psychiatrist, Ann Dally, finds that although many young women wonder whether they want to be mothers at all, for huge numbers, including many of those who are distressed and disturbed, bearing and rearing children is the most satisfying experience of their lives and it continues to be so despite the paradoxes and difficulties it entails; for some it may be the only satisfying experience they have ever known, says Dally.[4] Many other references in the published literature indicate women's deep love for children. Their love may be ambivalent, but it is strong.

So if most women love children and they continue to have strong maternal desires to have kids, why is motherhood today in a state of crisis? Why do we see a sharp decline in American birthrate, and why do so many women question whether to have children at all?

A Crisis of Motherhood

Never before in recorded history have so many bright young women chosen to postpone motherhood by fifteen or more years or give up maternity altogether. Although the United States still has a higher fertility rate than any other industrialized nation, about 2.012 children per woman (compared with six, seven or more children per woman in the past), this is only because of the large number of immigrants flocking into the country, who tend to produce comparatively large families. (The birthrate among white middle-class women is said to be significantly lower than the total national average.)

"For the first time in human history, mature women by the tens of thousands live the whole decade of their twenties—their most fertile years—entirely on their own: vulnerable and unprotected, lonely, and out of sync with their inborn nature. Some women positively welcome this state of affairs, but most do not, resenting the personal price they pay for their worldly independence," write Amy and Leon Kass of the University of Chicago.[5] We live in utterly novel and unprecedented times. One suspects that things were never the way they are, not here, not anywhere, they say. So the question is why? What is the cause for this sharp unprecedented change in women's lives and attitude toward motherhood? There are a number of societal reasons for this change in attitude and several personal reasons. It is important to understand these root causes when contemplating whether to have children or not.

"It's the economy" is one common oft-given response. It is expensive to raise kids today. A rising standard of living is often associated with a declining birthrate. And indeed, the American standard of living in recent years (until the onset of the current economic recession, which like all other recessions will probably be temporary) has been higher than ever before. Many young couples say that they cannot afford to have kids; and that women must work because it is impossible to support a family on only one salary. Yet people used to have larger families on a much smaller income and with a much lower standard of living.

Interestingly, an early twentieth century regional decline in birthrates among New England's WASPs caused Theodore Roosevelt to mock the WASPs' pretensions to "Puritan conscience," labeling their fecundity as "diseased" and "atrophied," according to Longman.[6] But the situation has only gotten much worse since then and it spread to the entire nation. So the roots of the problem of lower birthrate go deeper than a poor economy or some social disease. Let us take a few moments to consider:

CAUSES FOR THE DECLINING BIRTHRATE

The Move from Rural to Urban Lifestyle

As mentioned in Chapter One, the twentieth century saw the culmination of a century-long transition from an agrarian lifestyle to an urban/suburban one. This transition shifted the social weight from the extended family to the nuclear family; from life on the farm, surrounded by parents, grandparents, uncles, aunts, siblings, and cousins, all living and working nearby—to a family unit that includes, at best, only a father, mother, and two or three children, and increasingly, a large number of single-parent homes.

From a heavy reliance on children's helping hands with work on the farm—the more children the better—mother and children now spend a large part of the day alone at home (when not at work and at school), separated from their husband and father who works at a different, often distant, location—coming home only for the night.

Mothers and children no longer participate in the father's work. In most cases, children's work is no longer needed to help secure a family's income. Nor are today's children capable of contributing much to most parents' highly specialized job requirements. Their work is even legally prohibited today. Furthermore, children's assistance is no longer needed to secure one's economic situation in old age—as was often the case in the past—before mandatory retirement, bank savings, and pension funds were introduced.

This new social reality gives each generation the freedom to be independent and create its own lifestyle and economic base. Adult children are no longer obligated, or required, to carry on their parents' business. This reality has created tremendous opportunities and advantage. But it has also reduced the incentive and need to have many children. Once they no longer work with their parents, children stop being an economic asset. On the contrary, with today's requirement for higher education, and the tremendous cost that is associated with it, kids are increasingly becoming a major financial burden. Responsible couples, who may have even wished to have many children, are often compelled to limit the number of their offspring. Longman, for example, calculated that the average cost of raising a middle-class child born in the United States in 2001, from age 0 to 17, is $211,370. And this figure does not include any provision for college, nor does it take into account the potential loss in wages of a parent who stays home to take care of the child.

Contribution of Technology

It may be counterintuitive, but American technological ingenuity was another factor that contributed to the decline in the American birthrate. The many innovations that were developed during the early part of the twentieth century have significantly reduced the workload associated with home management, contributing to the changing nature of women's work at home. Consider how many hours of hard work were saved by the invention of the refrigerator, the dishwasher, the washing machine, permanent-press fabrics, processed foods, disposable diapers, and not less important, the supermarket, to name a few. These innovations enabled women to manage their households by themselves. There was no longer the need for many children, grandparents, aunts, or hired help to assist with basic household chores and home production of the many essentials for daily life.

Paradoxically, however, this overall positive development had its downside. Alone at home, with no other adults around, women grew increasingly lonely and bored. Separated from the hub of economic life, many women began experiencing a sense of alienation and discontent. Many became depressed. Others yearned to escape that loneliness and boredom. And these negative feelings, coupled with the reduced need for children, lowered women's desire to be at home, to have children and raise them. Yet there were additional reasons for the declining American birthrate.

The Birth Control Pill

The birth control pill was introduced to the public in the early 1960s. Although different contraceptive agents and devices have been used by men and women for millennia, these were never as convenient, reliable, or safe as Carl Djerassi's modern synthetic hormones-based oral contraceptive pill. The "pill" had a profound impact on the lives of women; and once women started using that pill, their lives changed in more ways than the size of their family. They began to experience a new sense of freedom—a new sense of control over their reproductive systems. Many women started feeling that they no longer needed the protection of marriage to be sexually active. This generated the idea of free love; the notion that women can now enjoy sex freely, like men, with no strings attached.

Spreading like wildfire during the 1970s, the idea of free love ushered in the sexual revolution. It became increasingly popular to postpone marriage, with its binding ties of loyalty and responsibility, in favor of "free" sexual experiences. Living together without marriage became pervasive. Motherhood, with its many responsibilities, was increasingly deferred by middle-class women until it was often too late to become pregnant. And the American birthrate began to sharply decline among the middle class, in favor of higher education, a career, and/or a more adventurous life.

The Women's Movement

Invigorated by these winds of freedom, and affected by the other developments mentioned above, the growing women's liberation movement was booming. Although several earlier waves of political women movements have come and gone in America, the period was ripe for new reforms, and the movement flourished, fueled by several books and articles written by women authors. *The Feminine Mystique,* by Betty Friedan, published in 1963, soon became a classic. So was *The Female Eunuch,* by Germaine Greer, published in 1971, as well as *MS* magazine, the brainchild of Gloria Steinem, launched in 1971

At first, the purpose of the movement was to help women find their way in the growing social unrest, discontent, and confusion that began to manifest with the socio-cultural changes described above. But instead of soothing frayed nerves, and explaining the growing sense of malaise to be the result of the new social condition—and the need to constructively adjust to these—the opposite has happened. The movement began to lash out against men, and make them the scapegoat. "Patriarchal" men were now denounced more than ever before as the source of all women's problems. Instead of adding tranquility, the movement began to tear women away from their homes, urging them to find paid employment opportunities outside the home, become less dependent on "oppressive" men—ideally financially and emotionally independent—and at last be free to fulfill their own personal dreams and aspirations.

Most of the movement's leaders were young—only a few were mothers—and they had little understanding of motherhood and what it involves, and they were often hostile to it. "Bringing up children is not a real occupation because children come up just the same, brought or not," wrote Germaine Greer in *The Female Eunuch,* as quoted by Ann Dallylly.[7] "It is easier to find out what feminists think about abortion, the female orgasm, rape, sexist education and the rights of lesbians than to find out what they think about motherhood," wrote Ann Dally in the 1980s.[8] As late as 2005,

Judith Warner wrote: "The feminist movement these days is all but silent on the issue of child care."[9]

With much publicity and psychological pressure, the movement has advocated the use of daycare centers to liberate women of their childcare responsibilities and give them the freedom to pursue their own dreams, aspirations, and personal fulfillment–"just like men." The movement looked down upon stay-at-home moms, viewing them as lazy nobodies, subserviently wasting their life on trivia, and therefore, as simply boring. "The hardest part about full-time parenting is the low esteem a segment of the women's movement has placed on nurturers who are unpaid. What a rotten thing for women to do to each other," said Maria Martinelli, mother of three, in the 1980s, as reported by the Dreskins.[10] The feminists' ambition was to deal with the larger issues of life–"just like men"–and change the world on a grand rather than small familial scale.

And the ground was fertile. The movement grew rapidly to become a significant political power, driving full speed ahead to change the fabric of American society; pitting women against men at home and in the workplace, inciting, during the 1970s and 1980s, the "war of the sexes," and pulling mothers away from their young children and their homes.

The movement succeeded in changing the dynamics at home, at the workplace, in the military, in the law, in schools and universities, and so on. Many women were swept away on the coattails of that movement. Many families were destroyed by the storm. Homes were broken. The lives of men were wrecked. The divorce rate began to skyrocket. The birthrate among the middle class declined. And the relationship between many mothers and their young children dramatically changed, for the worse. Growing numbers of young children began to be placed and raised in institutional daycare centers.

I lived through that period. I saw firsthand the damage and pain that it caused; the loss of trust between women and men; the fear of personal commitment; the anxiety about potential divorce; the rise in meaningless sex; and the loss of romance. No wonder that the rates of marriage and birth have sharply declined.

After the Storm

Fortunately, the wind has subsided. The storm has passed. The terrible AIDS epidemic has helped to curb the sexual revolution. The animosity between the genders has largely dissipated—the trust between men and women is slowly returning. Judith Warner even tells us that the women in her recent study reported that they have "wonderful husbands." But while many applaud the feminist movement's achievements, in particular the unprecedented access to rewarding work opportunities now open to women, "Four decades after the sexual revolution, nothing has worked out the way it was supposed to," concludes Maureen Dowd, the Pulitzer Prize winning columnist for the *New York Times*, and author of the provocative book *Are Men Necessary?*

As Dowd puts it: "Little did I realize that the sexual revolution would have the unexpected consequences of intensifying the confusion between the sexes. . . . It never occurred to me that the more women aped men, in everything from dress to orgasms, the more we would realize how inalienably different the sexes are."[11] "The sexes are circling each other as uneasily and comically as ever, from the bedroom to the boardroom to the Situation Room," says Dowd on the book's jacket. And Judith Warner, who is similarly disappointed by the movement's achievements, writes: "Feminism, filtered down and diluted by the mass media, came to be, not about a redefinition of motherhood or a reorganization of family life and society, but about questions of performance and control . . .'keep your laws off my body' became the rallying cry, not 'Let's change the body of law."[12] These are some of the larger

110

societal causes that have impacted women's maternal feelings leading to the decline in American birthrate. But there is another personal layer to the problem of declining birthrate, including a number of factors.

Personal Factors

a) Contemporary women have an overwhelming number of options to choose from that often conflict with the requirements of motherhood.

b) There is a great deal of misinformation concerning these options, which often lead to unrealistic expectations and poor decisions.

c) There is little or no guidance from family members, school officials, or social pundits how to choose wisely.

The net result of these factors is a state of confusion, often followed by a chain of mental and emotional problems. Hundreds of thousands of mothers who are conscious of the importance of what the women's movement is telling them, but who instinctively also recognize the importance of motherhood (though often with little understanding of what it actually involves), are anxious and confused. Aware that there is a conflict between motherhood and much of the feminist agenda, they contemplate motherhood with awe and uncertainty. "The prospect of becoming a mother now seems to many to be a tremendous step, a total change in life style, a fearful responsibility, an impossible expense, a frightening emotional commitment," wrote Ann Dally.[13] There is a "crisis of motherhood," she says. "Motherhood is not even appreciated," a high-powered single woman friend remarked to me. "Who has the time to have kids?" recounts Maureen Dowd about a New York publicist friend.

"Just taking care of her looks is a full-time job," she writes.[14] Let us take a look at what lies beneath the surface of these personal factors.

Too Many Options

It is not clear today what direction to take because all doors are now open for women as never before. We no longer have to model ourselves after our parents, as was the custom in the past. Every young adult has now the opportunity, even responsibility, to blaze his or her own path in life, choosing one out of many interesting possibilities. And almost any option is possible if one is willing to apply oneself and work hard for it, including whether or not to be a mother. This is exciting, even exhilarating, but it can also be scary and intimidating. It requires clarity of thought, introspection, some maturity, courage, and, most important, emotional freedom to choose; especially freedom from the influence of friends or from subliminal parental shackles that may hold one back.

Starting to carve out a life all by oneself, right out of high school, can indeed be a daunting experience. It can push some young women to escape into motherhood before they are actually ready for it (in or out of marriage), thus avoiding the need to take personal responsibility for other important decisions they need to make. On the other hand, fear can drive some young women away from motherhood for a long time—when important information is lacking and poor decisions are being made—until it may be too late to conceive or carry a pregnancy to full term.

Young women who are fortunate to have sensitive and more-or-less content mothers, who are able and willing to offer positive guidance, have a much easier time with their important life decisions. Unfortunately, many women today choose their path determined not to repeat their mothers' life. Many lived through their parents' divorces and are resolved to avoid a repeat of that pain. Many have seen a highly educated mother being miserable staying home to take care of her children, and they have decided to choose another way.

So instead of getting guidance from a more experienced mother, many women today find themselves quietly fighting the model she provided—searching alone for their own path. It is not surprising that Leslie Morgan Steiner, an executive with *The Washington Post* and the author of *Mommy Wars*, concluded her candid collection of women's essays stating that "It's no coincidence that so many women in this book wrote about their mothers and their childhoods. As mothers, we all, to various extents, carry the baggage of our pasts; we all try to re-create the good facets of our childhoods and to compensate for the painful ones."[15]

Misinformation and Fear of Divorce

Adding to the crisis of motherhood is a great deal of misinformation surrounding women's many options. Even an elementary question such as the optimal age range to become pregnant is obfuscated and with the answer often misleading. Important information about the effect of daylong use of daycare on the development of preschooler is often disseminated with a political agenda and bias. Lack of specific knowledge about the actual functions of motherhood, and fears about how it will change one's body, spirit, and mind, and affect a woman's relationship with her husband, all add to the crisis of motherhood. And so does the ever looming fear of divorce—so rampant today—which drives many women to pursue a career (often postponing marriage and/or children until it is too late) not necessarily because of immediate financial need, or love of a particular job, but as an insurance against divorce—to protect them, just in case, from sliding into possible poverty. There is nothing wrong, of course, with a woman's career plans and aspirations, but these should be made with careful consideration of all the other important aspects and desires of her life.

Poor Guidance

I know a highly educated, respected, and long-married couple, with two beautiful bright daughters, whose life story encapsulates today's crisis of motherhood. The girls were encouraged by their stay-at-home mom from an early age to become competent professionals–so that they'll be able to take care of themselves. (You cannot rely today on a husband, the mother explained). Both girls were ambitious and diligent students. One daughter became a successful physician, the other a successful accountant. One daughter is now in her early forties and the younger is in her early thirties, both are unmarried so far. They are now financially secure and independent, but the mother is worried about their future loneliness. "How can it be that such a normal family finds itself in such an abnormal situation," she quipped to me one day in a telephone conversation.

Lonely, stressed, and prone to depressive moods, each daughter has a dog. "The dogs are their children," the mother candidly bemoaned, admitting that she herself cares for the dogs as if they were her grandchildren. She often leaves her husband alone, for days at a time, flying out of town to visit the girls who live in other cities, to help them out with different problems. The latest I have heard is that the older daughter, the one who is the accountant, gave birth to a boy out of wedlock. "She does not want to marry the father of the child," the happy grandmother related; happy to finally have a grandchild (her first), and for the fact that her daughter will no longer be alone. "Things are moving in the right direction," she cryptically explained. Yet I wonder. I wish them all well but I can't stop thinking that this is just another example of the current crisis of motherhood. How self-fulfilling one's attitudes toward life can be.

Although this mother is very dedicated and well-meaning, I wonder if the advice she gave her daughters was not driven more by fear (her own fear of divorce, in this case) than by judicious planning. She may have also lacked some of the information described in this book—specifically in the following pages—a common want today, and one of the reasons for writing this book.

A National Perspective

One other factor to consider when contemplating motherhood is the national need. Americans are not used to think in these terms. Being founded on individualism, we often neglect to consider the general good. But in addition to the six reasons to have children described in Chapter 2 there is another demographic-economic overlay to this issue. American economy has been based on the idea of population growth; that a growing population is the source of economic growth. More people create more demand for the products and services that are being sold, and these demands increase the labor force that manufactures those products and services. But as Phillip Longman, a senior fellow at the New America Foundation, eloquently analyzes, while our day-to-day experiences and the impressions we gather from the media, continue to suggest a growing population, that may even threaten the quality of our life, this is only the result of immigration. A look beneath the surface of events shows the dramatic decline in the American birthrate.[16]

The current U.S. birthrate is about 2.0125 children per woman,[17] which is below the level required to replace the population. Some would argue that there is nothing wrong with that figure, since there are enough people to meet all our needs. However, a declining population is associated with the aging of that population. While people are growing older, not enough are being born to replace them. "Between 2005 and 2025, the population aged 65 and older will swell by more than 72 percent, according to Census Bureau projections," writes Longman.[18] Fewer workers will then be available to produce the goods and services needed by the American public; in particular by the growing segment of older retirees who will increasingly require more specialized services. We are all familiar with the ongoing debates about healthcare and social security. The demographic projections are, therefore, increasingly worrisome.

It is unlikely that Americans will start again to produce large families as in past generation. Children are expensive; mothers have interesting careers outside the home; people want to have freedom to enjoy life; to name a few reasons. But if America is to maintain its standard of living and meet future social, economic, health, education, and military obligations, we must at least maintain the size of our native population. While America has always welcomed controlled legal immigration, to continuously rely mainly on immigrants to supply the country's basic labor needs, as happened in Western Europe, will be national suicide. An average of two or three well- developed children per woman is therefore, needed to secure the future optimal size and well-being of American society. The emphasis is on well-developed children. The sad reality is that underdeveloped or poorly developed children, as lovable as they may be, often constitute a drain on the economy. While every society has its share of youngsters who will never achieve productive adulthood—for a variety of reasons—and these children must be loved and cared for as all other children, a highly developed culture strives to minimize the size of this group as much as possible through prevention and good education (see chapter 4 for details).

SO SHOULD EVERY WOMAN BECOME A MOTHER?

The Need to Be Ready for Motherhood

Young women must be clear about the difference between mother and motherhood. They are not one and the same. The word "mother" describes the biological state of having given birth to a child. The word "motherhood" describes the cultural process of raising that child. The first may be attractive, the second is hard work. All mammals have mothers—the female member of the species that gives birth to their young. But we never talk about mammalian motherhood. "Mother" is, one of the oldest words in all languages. "Motherhood," on the other hand, is relatively a new term. According to Dally, the

Oxford English Dictionary contains no reference to "motherhood" earlier than 1597, when the term first emerged.[19]

In many cultures throughout history the mother figure was worshiped like a deity; perceived to be the source of all good that could do no harm. In recent years, however, we have come to realize that not all mothers are good. While a mother is a mother, whether she is good or not so good depends on her motherly skills, her feelings toward her child, and her understanding of the culture's expectations of her maternal functions (see chapter 4 for details). It is very easy to become a mother (especially for young women in their twenties), but it is very demanding to be involved in the daily process of motherhood. Young women need, therefore, to distinguish between the two concepts and take the necessary time to reflect on when they are truly ready for motherhood.

Before you become a mother you have to deeply want to be a mother. You have to know what motherhood involves, and you need to have the means (both emotional and material) to provide the basic needs of your child—physical, socio-emotional, and mental. "Those who do not want children or who are not able or willing to commit themselves to them in the way our present society demands, are better off without them," wrote Dally.[20] Parenthood is a serious and very hard work. It should only be embarked on by those who take it seriously and who are prepared to give a great deal of themselves to it. If this puts some young people off it altogether it may be a good thing, she added.

So my short answer to this chapter's opening question is NO. Not every woman should become a mother. One first needs to be ready for this all-encompassing, exhilarating, and life-giving experience. This answer, however, is not written in stone. It is fluid, subjective, and prone to change. A woman who is not ready for motherhood at one point in her life may be ready later on. In fact, most American women are not ready for motherhood at the period when they are capable of becoming a mother, biologically speaking. A healthy twelve- to thirteen- year-old girl can get pregnant and give birth to a child. She will then be a teenage mother. But she is not ready for motherhood in our society. She does not have the means to raise a child, nor is she emotionally and mentally capable of bringing up that child to a healthy, productive maturity. She herself still needs substantial time to grow, develop, and mature.

In twenty-first century America, where women have the freedom to take any path they desire (unlike in less developed societies where a woman who deviates from the cultural norm may be severely punished, or even killed), women must be especially responsible, beginning at puberty, to honestly assess when and if they are ready for motherhood. Teen-age girls should be guided and advised by more mature women, ideally their mothers, or another trusted family member. Women (often girls) who step into motherhood casually, accidentally, or without preparation and thought are hurting their own futures as well as that of their children, in addition to potentially becoming a burden on society.

The Age Factor

One of the most important facts to remember is that a woman's window of opportunity to become pregnant, with no complications and minimal cost is relatively short. The prime childbearing years are between ages twenty to thirty. According to the American College of Obstetricians and Gynecologists, in June 2000, fertility "starts to decline in a woman's late 20s and early 30s and decreases even more after age 35." Sylvia Ann Hewlett, the founding president of the Center for Work-Life Policy, is even more specific, saying that "fertility drops 50 percent after age 35, and 95 percent after age 40." While 72 percent of twenty- eight- year-old women get pregnant after trying for a year, only 24 percent of thirty- eight- year-olds do, she says.[21]

This information may surprise many, who grew up like me, with the notion that women are fertile so long as they haven't reached menopause. I still recall my surprise, not too long age, when I first heard from a gynecologist, a fertility expert I met at one of my grandsons birthday party, that women past age 35 have a hard time to conceive, and that many need (often choose) to get a fresh egg from a younger donor.

And yet in recent years women have been led to believe that new medical procedures will help them conceive and give birth to a healthy baby into their fifties, and even sixties. As Sylvia Ann Hewlett puts it: "Misled by the media, which loves to hype miracle babies, and lulled into a false sense of security by an infertility industry eager to profit from late-in-life babies, too many young women now believe that assisted reproductive technology (ART) has let them off the hook. . . . They feel that they can quite literally rewind the biological clock."[22] In reality however, according to Hewlett, the average forty-something woman trying to get pregnant for the first time faces daunting odds no matter how hard she tries, or how much she spends. And if she is lucky and gets pregnant at this age, she faces a 50 to 80 percent chance of losing her baby through miscarriage. "Over 90 percent of late-in-life pregnancies involve IVF (in vitro fertilization), with prices ranging from $10,000 to $100,000, depending on how many attempts are required and whether or not you need donor eggs," writes Hewlett.[23]

Also Eve Mason Ekman, a medical social worker in San Francisco, relates how many of the women she interviewed, who had waited to have children, reported that "though there appears to be infinite choice in family planning with modern contraception and fertilization techniques, there is still significant difficulty, if not failure, when trying to conceive later in the reproductive years."[24]

So age continues to be a major factor to consider by women who want children, despite the availability of new medical procedures and interventions. Although they are healthier and live much longer than women in previous generations, today's women appear to be less fertile than their mothers were, even factoring in the impact of new technologies. Several reasons may explain this fact:

According to Hewlett, today's women are likely to have had several sexual partners and therefore experience a much higher incidence of pelvic inflammatory disease, which creates scar tissue that can block the fallopian tubes and cause fertility problems. Today's women are also more stressed than were women in previous generations, having less stable marriages, and trying to establish financial and professional independence, in addition to handling their family responsibilities. Stress, as we all know, can affect a woman's hormonal state, often decreasing her body's readiness to conceive.

But most important, by starting to have children at a later age than was customary in the past (often after thirty rather than at twenty), women miss out on their prime fertility years—when their eggs are still fresh and their hormonal state is all primed for pregnancy. (The muscles of the uterus, like the muscles of any other body organ, apparently need to be activated and used early—at what appears to be a critical period–or else they will atrophy.)

Bernadine Healy, former director of NIH and the American Red Cross warns about another looming pediatric crisis. At every year recently over "half a million babies (are) coming into the world weeks to months before they should," she says in a U.S. News & World Report article.[25] The United States spends $5.8 billion–about a quarter of all expenditures for pediatric hospitalization—on the care of neonates (leading the world, on that). But many of the preemies that survive "confront health problems later, like asthma or developmental disorders." There are known risk factors that lead to problem pregnancies, says Healy, and many of these are controllable, including smoking, drug abuse, uterine infections, teen pregnancy, middle- age pregnancy, and fertility treatments. This information needs to be broadly disseminated. Women of child-bearing age ought to take these factors into account.

One other age-related point to consider when contemplating motherhood is the high energy level required to raise young children. Chasing a preschooler at age twenty-five feels very different from chasing that same child at forty. I could not say it better than Wendy Mogel, a clinical psychologist in Los Angeles, who described her own feelings in a parenting book: "I worried most at night about my age. I had Susanna when I was thirty-five and Emma when I was thirty-nine and I couldn't help calculating the future. . . . When Emma is twenty-one I'll be sixty. If I were younger, would I have more energy for them? How old will I be when my daughters marry? Will I be seventy? Will I be breathing? None of my friends is likely to see her grandchildren married. What have we done?"[26]

Good Parental Advice

Women should start thinking of these age-related issues at the beginning of their adult life rather than leave it to when they are 30. Ideally, they should begin thinking about these factors as early as in high school, when they start to contemplate their future education and career paths. Parents and high school counselors have an important role to play by raising these issues with senior teens and start discussing them. Some will say that teenagers do not like to think about these matters, being only interested in fun and sex. Yet babies, motherhood, fatherhood, and childcare are too important a topic to leave to chance. Once teenagers can become sexually active they need specific information about the subject, and knowledge about the implications of certain types of behavior.

While it is true that teenagers are not particularly contemplative, they do seek correct information and they are eager to hear honest and serious advice, in particular from their parents, if they have a good relationship with them. We underestimate them and cut them short when we deprive them of our best advice. And we cannot expect them to mature and behave responsibly if we are not mature enough ourselves to take the responsibility to enlighten and guide them.

I will never forget my discussion many years ago with my then fourteen- year-old son. A friend of his, a girl, came over to the house one day and the two teenagers sat talking in the living room. While I was preparing dinner in the kitchen, I noticed that things were getting a little too hot in the living room. The fourteen- year-old girl was way too mature for my son and I felt that, as the mother, I needed to give the boy some beginning sex education, to avoid future trouble. When the girl left, I called my son to the kitchen table and started giving him the ABCs of sexual behavior with some basic facts and straight advice. We talked for some four hours, at the end of which my son had tears in his eyes, and said, "Thank you, Mom, for talking to me about this topic. I know it was difficult for you to talk about that and it just showed me how much you care about me. Thank you." Many years have passed since that incident, but it is still fresh in my mind (including where we sat at that kitchen table). And I will probably never forget it.

Young women who know that they want to have children, and give birth naturally with minimal complications and cost, would be wise to plan on having their first child no later than in their late twenties. This advice may conflict with their professional plans, but there is no smart responsible way around the biological fact. If one wants to have children naturally, with minimal complications and cost, it is wisest to work with biology rather than against it; Instead of viewing one's gender as a shackle, women should accept their femininity as a glorious manifestation of nature (or God). "Why do women not see that in motherhood lies their power?" asks Dally. It is only their weakness when they allow it to be denigrated and neglected, as it is at present, she says.[27]

A woman's body in her twenties, is the most primed to conceive and give birth to a healthy baby. Subsequent pregnancies can occur at a later age, but it is important to start the reproductive system working when it is at its prime, to prevent reproductive organs from weakening.

This advice also implies that young women who want to have children, with no complications and minimal cost, would be wise to invest the time during their twenties, in addition to furthering their education, also in serious romance and finding their life partner. By delaying serious love and marriage to after one is professionally established, women decrease their chance to conceive naturally and give birth to a healthy well-developed baby. They also decrease the pool of suitable potential mates. They enter, what Mason and Ekman (the mother and daughter team of a university dean and a medical social worker) dub the professional Make-or-Break Years between thirty to forty; The decade when careers take off or flounder, when "all professions require a time commitment that clashes with the possibility of family formation.[28]

In summary, you have to be ready for motherhood (and fatherhood) before you become a parent—physically, emotionally, mentally, and financially. This implies that responsible couples (especially the woman), should avoid getting pregnant as long as they do not have the ability and the means to provide their babies with basic physical, emotional, and mental needs.

One does not need to have a high standard of living to be a good parent. Few people have full financial security in their early years of marriage. Nor should one think that a young couple will stop to grow and develop. People continue to mature throughout their lives, and a young married couple can continue to grow and develop together. But a couple planning to become parents need to be sufficiently mature in character, responsible in nature, and possess attitudes that are conducive for parenthood. An unplanned pregnancy, in twenty-first- century America, is either an accident or the consequence of irresponsibility. The next chapter discusses a novel solution for the motherhood/career conflict.

CHAPTER SEVEN

A NEW PARADIGM FOR AMERICAN MOTHERHOOD

We began to realize how discouraged and overwhelmed many Gen-X/Y women felt and how infrequently they revealed their self-doubt and confusion. . .about the direction in which their lives are heading.

–Macko and Rubin, *Midlife Crisis at 30*

The Conflict

Women find it difficult today to establish a comfortable balance between family responsibilities and professional life. At no time is this conflict deeper than when preschool children are involved. Many women view this conflict as an either-or situation. They feel guilty when they decide to stop being a full-time mother to a young preschooler, or conversely, experience frustration for having wasted their education (sometimes a very expensive education) if they lower their professional aspirations to become a stay-at-home mom. While several solutions for this dilemma have been discussed in chapter 3, mostly increasing the father's childcare responsibilities, I would like to propose another solution, based on a different paradigm.

The Solution

Life expectancy in twenty-first- century America is between seventy-five to eighty years. This means that the average length of one's life as an adult is about sixty years. Men have accepted the fact that they may have to change their professional specialty several times during their lifetime. Staying with one company, or field, for one's life's duration, as was customary in previous generations, is hardly an option today.

In response to this reality, the American educational system, has been preparing today's students to be lifelong learners.

I propose that women adopt a similar view toward work as do men and be ready to change functions over their life span. Motherhood is one of the most exhilarating and profound experiences a woman can have. To be a mother and raise two or three healthy and happy family members and future citizens is probably the most important job a woman can do. Since maternal responsibilities are most demanding when children are in their preschool years, I propose that women devote about ten years—just one sixth of their sixty years of adult life—to "intense mothering," that is, a period in which they give birth to and raise two or three children through their early formative years, before they resume, or start, their paid professional career. This special decade could be considered their "intense mothering period," or the Bonding Years period.

Having such a plan in mind, a life roadmap of sort, women will be less conflicted. Knowing that their decade of intense mothering is just a distinct phase in their life, not all of it—perhaps their most important phase, but one that will not necessarily crush their professional aspirations—they will have greater appreciation for this period, and be more relaxed to enjoy it. Moreover, they will have the time to prepare themselves (if necessary, with additional education and training) for their professional career. Disciplined women could still achieve a great deal in the outside world during the next fifty years of adult life left to them. There are many examples of high achieving women who have followed just this kind of path. So let us take a look at some of these examples:

Three Examples

Consider former Secretary of State Madeleine Albright, one of the highest-ranking women in the history of U.S. government, and the first woman to hold the post of Secretary of State. She was born in Prague at the eve of World War II, and found refuge in America with her parents, who settled in Denver when she was 11, and became U.S. citizen at 20. She attended Wellesley College, majoring in political science; married Joseph Patterson Albright and the couple had three daughters. For many years, Madeline Albright focused on raising her daughters, while slowly taking courses, including graduate work at Columbia University, receiving her doctorate degree in public law and government at age 39. Only then, at 39, did she begin her paid career in academia and politics—after her three daughters were in school.[1]

She joined the National Security Council, became an ambassador to the United Nations, then a professor at Georgetown University and foreign policy expert before her nomination to be Secretary of State. Interestingly, her daughters are mothers themselves by now and all have professional careers, yet they structure their schedule differently. One daughter is a banker, and two are lawyers. One started a law firm with another woman to have greater work flexibility. Another works full time, and the third, following a period of maternity leave, works a flexible schedule. "Women's lives don't go in a straight line, they zigzag all over the place," told Madeleine Albright to a *Time* magazine reporter in 1997, according to Wendy Sachs.[2]

Next we have Congresswoman Nita Lowey from New York who was first elected to the U.S. House of Representatives in 1988 and is now serving her eleventh term. She has the reputation of being one of the most influential members of Congress. Married close to 50 years to Stephen Lowey, she has three grown children and eight grandchildren. Though a natural politician, and very active, she did not run for office until she was 50, and didn't do any paid work until her youngest child was 9 years old. "I think it's very difficult to have it all at the same time, but life is a cycle", said Lowey in an interview with Wendy Sachs. "For me raising children was very important. I think it would be very difficult to do this job while my children were young." Her recommendation to young mothers: "Enjoy your children; they are only babies once."[3]

And then we have Sandra Day O'Connor, the first woman to serve as United States Supreme Court Justice. A graduate of Stanford University, magna cum laude, who received her LL.D from Stanford two years later at age 32. Yet she was unable to find a position in a private law firm, because she was a woman—though she did get one offer to work as a secretary. Married to John Jay O'Connor, the couple had three sons, and for a few years she focused on raising the children. She returned to work on a part-time basis as an assistant attorney general for Arizona when her younger son was 3 years-old. She served in different capacities since then, including being a state senator, majority leader, judge on a County Superior Court, before President Reagan announced her, at age 51, as his appointee to the Supreme Court, determined to have a woman in that position. She resigned from this life-long position after close to 30 years of service, to spend more time with her ailing husband.[4]

There are many more examples of women who stayed home to raise their kids during their formative preschool years, and still succeeded to achieve a high professional standing. Life is long enough to do both functions well. But this requires flexibility, the right attitude, and stamina. Whether a woman's path in life zig-zags as Madeleine Albright described, or goes in a cycle as Nita Lowey remarked, it is long enough to be able to devote the necessary time for young children's development, and then take on a worthwhile professional responsibility.

A Cultural Shift

However, women must have the backing and appreciation of their husbands to be able to fully carry their maternal responsibility. They also need to feel the support and appreciation of American culture. American culture needs to rethink its view about the motherhood/career conflict. It needs to rise above the current chaotic condition, where there is no culturally recognized custom or guideline how to handle the motherhood/career conflict, and clarify its goals for early childhood development, as well as its expectations of women. Most importantly, American culture as a whole needs to recognize the important role that mothers have in their young children's upbringing and its irreplaceable quality for the children and for the nation. Let us recall again Teddy Roosevelt's wise statement, mentioned earlier, that a mother's work with her children is more important than the work of any man no matter how important his function. Roosevelt's statement could not be more cogent in today's world. America will benefit by incorporating this view into its core cultural mores.

And so I call for a *cultural shift* in attitude toward the motherhood/career conflict. I propose that young women establish a ten year period of intense mothering, during their children's preschool years, i.e. the Bonding Years period, in which they give birth to two or three children and focus on the kids' development, stimulating and facilitating their optimal foundation for growth. At the same time, I challenge the American culture to show greater appreciation for women who choose to stay home for a decade to raise their young kids, and once their period of intense mothering is over, make it easier for them to return to work or start their path in the professional world. These women are likely to be more mature, responsible, less conflicted, better worker, and overall a better long-time investment for their employer than younger beginners. Like in the three examples described above, such women will have a rich, guilt-free, and more relaxed full life, with the necessary time to establish a better balance between motherhood and career; a balance that works best for them.

I am certain that some will criticize me at this point for being a Pollyanna, ignoring the large number of children growing up in divorced families and single-parent homes, under conditions where the mother has to go out to work and find some alternative for her care. I am well aware of this unfortunate situation. But the intended primary audiences for this book are young women at the beginning of their adult life, when all options are still open for them, and mothers of teenage daughters who wish to help and guide them how to make wise decisions for their life. One must clarify to them the relevant issues they'll have to deal with, so that they, and you, could decide with confidence, on the best path for you and your daughters' life. I also hope that this book will stir a national debate on these important issues.

Most women want to have children. Most men want to have children. American society wants and needs children. And we all want these children to be healthy in body and mind. Yet children need good parents. "Without adequate mothering the world becomes intolerable," wrote Ann Dally.[5] And they develop best when they have a father and a mother who live together in harmony. Parenting is a serious job. Couples need to be ready for parenthood, and not have children when they are not ready or able to properly take care of them. Once they have their kids, they need to do their best to provide them with a good environment in which to grow and develop. This is one of the most important functions of both men and women living in a healthy advanced society.

CHAPTER EIGHT

IS MARRIAGE NECESSARY?

*Marriage is and remains the most important voyage of discovery
a human being undertakes.*

—**Kierkegaard,** *Reflections on Marriage*

Marriage under Attack

We now come to the topic of marriage. Marriage has a profound impact on a woman's way of life and the environment she can provide for her growing children. Yet the institution of marriage is today under attack and undergoing fundamental transformations. When we have about a third of U.S. children born every year to unwed mothers (1,641,700 in 2006) is marriage still necessary? It is important to gain insight into this basic social organization in a book that discusses motherhood and how best to raise young children.

From the days that humans formed structured societies, in most periods and places, including until a generation ago also in America, marriage was part of the normal life cycle of most, if not all, young adults. Different forms of marriage existed within different societies and cultures. Customs, ceremonies, and laws varied. Some men would occasionally ask, "Why marry?" But there was never, until very recently, a cultural debate about the institution of marriage itself or its merits. People got married because their parents were married, the culture expected them to get married, and there was a general agreement that marriage is desirable and beneficial for both the individual and society at large.

The universality of marriage was traditionally attributed to the many social and personal functions it performed. Marriage regulated procreation and sexual gratification; the care of children, their education and socialization; the protection of women; the line of descent; the division of labor between the sexes; property rights; and provision for the satisfaction of personal needs for affection, status, and companionship. Because of the importance of these functions, marriage has always been legally, religiously, and socially sanctioned. And the institution of marriage was remarkably stable. Until a few decades ago, it was difficult in America to obtain a divorce and practically impossible without good reasons such as adultery, abandonment, abuse, or alcoholism. In 1880, only one marriage in twenty one–fewer than 5 percent—ended in divorce, according to historian Robert L. Griswold.[1]

Yet this long-standing stability of marriage has been dramatically shaken in recent decades, especially since the 1980s, in most Western societies. We live in a revolutionary time when all things are being questioned. Many traditional values, customs, and laws are now being challenged, changed, or altogether discarded. And marriage is no exception. The brush fire that scorched the social landscape has touched also the nuptial bond, shaking its very nature and purpose.

A number of factors have contributed to the changing attitude toward marriage. Including among these are the equal employment opportunities for women since the mid-1960s, and their growing financial independence; the invention of the pill which enabled women to have easy access to sexual gratification with little responsibility or negative consequence; the smaller size of the American family; the social acceptance of out-of-wedlock births; and, perhaps, most important, the easy availability of divorce—especially after the adoption of "no-fault" divorce in almost every state—and the overall higher expectations of marriage. All these factors weakened the need for marriage, making it less indispensable.

Today, it is estimated that between 40 percent and 50 percent of U.S. marriages will end in divorce, according to Census Bureau statistics and the National Center for Health.[2] Thirty seven percent of American children are now born out of wedlock to single-parent moms, according to Mike Stobbe of the Associated Press.[3] This means that out of 4.1 million babies born in the United States in 2005, more than 1.5 million were offspring of unmarried women. Recent figures suggest that almost 70 percent of black children are born out of wedlock, says Clarence Page,[4] and according to Heather MacDonald, nearly half of the children born to Hispanic mothers in the United States are illegitimate.[5]

While the rate of births among unwed teenage mothers has declined slightly, the rate of births among older unwed women has risen, according to Herbert Klein, a research fellow at the Hoover Institution.[6] More women in their thirties and forties, hearing their biological clock ticking, choose to give birth despite their single status. And it has become more acceptable in today's society to have a child without getting married.

This is alarming, especially in view of the reported higher likelihood of social pathology among children who grow up in single-mother households.[7] This situation may create a new American underclass that is fast growing and producing more juvenile delinquents, more school failure, more welfare use, and more teen pregnancy in the future.

Of little consolation is the fact that other Western societies experience a similar situation. In France, for example, it is estimated that 43 percent of marriages will end in divorce, in Germany 41 percent, in the United Kingdom 53 percent, in Sweden 64 percent; in Belgium 56 percent, and so on. This rate of family breakdown is stunning. And "Why marry?" is no longer a question for the few: it is now a question for the culture as a whole. As Amy and Leon Kass, of the University of Chicago, put it, "Today, it is marriage, rather than the single life, that is on the defensive."[8] The question is why? (Ironically, the current economic recession may have some positive effect on marriage, lowering the rate of divorce. Divorce is expensive and in difficult economic times fewer people can afford it).

Arguments against Marriage

Middle-class men are apparently fearful of financial burdens, emotional commitment, and loss of freedom. Women worry about loss of independence, submitting to inequality and "patriarchy," and slowing their career development. In addition, men and women who have experienced the painful breakup of their parents' marriages are reluctant to repeat the same experience in their own lives, and tend to shy away from, or postpone, getting married until they are sure of their choice and decision. Many of these young adults, who may cohabit, ask, "Why marry now?" "What's so important about the marriage ceremony and certificate?"

And who can blame them? Why should a healthy, ambitious young man, full of energy and drive to accomplish, marry a woman whose top priority is to establish her own independent and full-fledged career? This means placing future children in a daycare center to be raised by a succession of strangers, or taking into the household another woman to be his children's nanny.

Why should he marry, when the romantic love a couple may feel for each other might change after the honeymoon is over and the stresses of daily life appear? Why should he marry when sexual activity and love are confused, cohabitation is widespread and condoned, and one can easily establish a "relationship," including sexual intimacy with no commitment and strings attached. "All the attractive intelligent young women I date are feminists," lamented a young unmarried physician a few years ago. "I have a hard time finding an intelligent woman that looks forward to being a wife, a mother, and creating a warm family home," he added. Why should he marry, when the possibility of no-fault divorce with its severe emotional toll and disastrous financial consequences will always loom in the background? When as a single man he has much greater freedom and more money for personal luxury items and experiences?

From the woman's perspective, the questions are somewhat similar. Although women have been traditionally more eager to marry than men, they, too, are now asking "Why marry? Or why marry now?" Raised and educated like boys, with no special consideration to their biology and gender inclinations, today's girls are told they can do anything that boys can do. Moreover, they are expected by the culture, often even pushed, to do so. In stark contrast to the not so distant past, and in the name of progress and women's rights, girls are now encouraged by teachers and often by their own parents to suppress any inkling of gender difference, considering it to be a weakness, a dated attitude, a thing of the past.

Romantic love, marriage to a man who is, or soon will be, the main financial provider, raising children, and establishing a warm home environment—where values are being discussed and transmitted, character is shaped and formed, and physical and emotional nurturing are provided—used to be a woman's dream and primary focus in life. Outside work, community service, and intellectual/artistic activities used to take second place, as needed or desired and as time permitted. But today's women are encouraged to establish their separate emotional and economic identity outside their family, often blaming the economy for forcing them to go out to work when young children are involved. Moreover, today's women are frequently judged and valued by their personal achievements beyond family.

And so young women are told to get an education in order to find a good job that will help them cover their expenses, aid the family finances, and provide financial security in case of future divorce. (Some women consider their professional work to be a Divorce Insurance.) As a result, many talented women today are as ambitious and driven in the workplace as men. They are doing their best to reach the very top in their field, pushing marriage and children aside until they reach their desired professional peak. Many women do not realize that by then they may be less attractive to men as potential spouses. The older they become, and the higher they climb on the career ladder, the less desirable they become as mates. "The aroma of male power is an aphrodisiac for women, but the perfume of female power is a turnoff for men," writes Maureen Dowd, the Pulitzer Prize-winning columnist for the *New York Times*.[9]

Thus many women are also asking "Why marry? Or, why marry now?" Why be distracted from a promising fast career track by the responsibilities of marriage, commitment to a husband, and the care of children? Why marry, when today's women can be financially independent, have a job they enjoy, and easy access to a "relationship," including sexual intimacy, with no commitment or strings attached"—just like men?"

What a difference a few decades can make. People used to be anchored in family; today many are anchored in a demanding career. They used to be home-and-family centered; today many are centered in their professional work, placing their primary focus, energy, and attention on that. "Work is my life," remarked a woman CEO of a large, famous corporation, even though she is married and the mother of two young daughters. But are people any happier today? Have the last decades of social achievements improved their lives? Are children doing better under our current shaky marital conditions? And what is going to be the future of marriage given these circumstances?

The Pendulum Swings Back

"Women moving up still strive to marry up. Men moving up still tend to marry down," writes Maureen Dowd.[10] The two sexes going in opposite directions have led to an epidemic of professional women missing out on husbands and kids. "Four decades after feminism blossomed in a giddy wave of bra barbecues, birth-control pills and unisex clothes, the ideal of having it all is a visible cliché," adds Dowd.[11] Journalists Lia Macko and Kerry Rubin, speaking for many, declare that we are a generation in the middle of a midlife crisis at thirty. More women enter therapy at age thirty, they say, than at any other point in their lives.[12] Women become frustrated and depressed about their inability to meet their expectations of having it all— including a great career, a fabulous marriage, and beautiful kids–by thirty. Their "fantasies and expectations of what adult life looks like clash with the reality of what adult life *is* like" quote Macko and Rubin from Yale psychologist Daniel Levinson.[13]

Fully 75 percent of twenty-five to thirty-five year-old women say that their professional lives interfere with their personal lives, and more than a third state that the conflict is very severe, report Macko and Rubin. "We've hit the New Glass Ceiling—one that keeps women who want a life outside of work from getting ahead and doesn't allow women who are getting ahead to have a life outside the office," they say.[14] These two hard-driving journalists soon realized that the "nonnegotiable" demands of work were interfering with the nonnegotiable and much more important demands of being a friend, wife, daughter, and woman. "We knew our lives were horribly out of sync," they write.[15]

But life apparently has a way of working itself out. After forty years of active feminism, with millions of women having entered the workforce (either full-time or part- time), and thousands of children spending significant parts of their early years away from their parents—often cared for by less-educated strangers—the pendulum appears slowly to swing back. Many women are reassessing their lives, reevaluating their options, and changing direction again. Wiser, with forty years of experience having played out before their eyes and with a front-row seat from which to observe the social chaos around them, there is a sobering new realization.

Generation X/Y women no longer question whether they can become CEOs, neurosurgeons, or senators. They know that they can. The question that confronts them now is at what cost do women reach these positions? A remarkably high percentage of Gen-X mothers are now quitting their jobs to stay at home with their kids. According to a U.S. 2000 census, thirty to thirty-five year-old college-educated women have sparked the largest exodus of working mothers from the workplace since 1976.[16]

Arguments for Marriage

There appears to be a return to the hearth. Women who used to loath the possibility of a "Mommy track" are now praying for it, observes Maureen Dowd.[17] There is also a return to romance, and a desire to make marriage work. As Dowd writes, "In a world where many women either get divorced or never got married, it is now a status symbol to snag a married name. . . . Nowadays most young brides want to take their husband's name and brag on the moniker Mrs., a brand that proclaims you belong to him. T-shirts with Mrs. emblazoned in sequins or sparkly beads are popular wedding shower gifts," she says.[18]

So what is the appeal of marriage in this day and age, following forty years of active feminism with its sweeping social achievements? And does it matter to children if their parents are officially married? It is interesting to read the advice of none other than Charles Darwin—written as he was debating this very issue before his 1839 marriage to Emma Wedgwood. Darwin's handwritten note (published by Nora Barlow, Darwin's granddaughter, in the appendix to her edition of Darwin's autobiography) shows that although "Why marry?" is a widespread contemporary question, it has occasionally been raised also by thinking individuals in the past. Headed "This is the Question," the charming note gives us insight into Darwin's nineteenth century thought process.[19] Following is the text of this note:

THIS IS THE QUESTION

MARRY

Children—(if it please God)—constant companion, (friend in old age) who will feel interested in one, object to be beloved and played with—better than a dog anyhow—
Home, and someone to take care of house—
Charms of music and female chit-chat. These things good for one's health. Forced to visit and receive relations *but terrible loss of time.*

My God, it is intolerable to think of spending one's whole life, like a neuter bee, working, working and nothing after all.—

No, no won't do.—
Imagine living all one's day solitarily in smoky dirty London House.—
Only picture to yourself a nice soft wife on a sofa with good fire, and books and music perhaps—compare this vision with the dingy reality of Great Marlboro' St.
Marry—Marry—Marry

NOT MARRY

No children, (no second life) no one to care for in old age —
What use of working without sympathy from near and dear friends —
who are near and dear friends to the old except relatives.
Freedom to do what one likes — Choice of Society *and little* of it.
Conversation of clever men at clubs, -

Not forced to visit relatives, and to bend at every trifle — to have the expense and anxiety of children — perhaps quarreling.
Loss of time — cannot read in the evenings-fatness and idleness - anxiety and responsibility — less money for books, etc — if many children to gain one's bread. — (But then it is very bad for one's health to work too much)
Perhaps my wife won't like London; then the sentence is banishment and degradation with indolent idle fool —

On the reverse side of Darwin's note is the following summation:
It being proved necessary to marry—when? Soon or late. The Governor says soon for otherwise bad if one has children—one's character is more flexible—one's feelings more lively, and if one does not marry soon, one misses so much good pure happiness.—
But then if I married tomorrow: there would be an infinity of trouble and expense in getting and furnishing a house—fighting about no Society—morning calls—awkwardness—loss of time every day—(without one's wife was an angel and made one keep

industrious)—Then how should I manage all my business if I were obliged to go every day walking with my wife.—Eheu!! I never should know French,—or see the Continent,—or go to America, or go up in a Balloon, or take solitary trip in Wales—poor slave, you will be worse than a negro—And then horrid poverty (without one's wife better than an angel and had money)—Never mind my boy—Cheer up—One cannot live this solitary life, with groggy old age, friendless and cold and childless staring one in one's face, already beginning to wrinkle. Never mind, trust to chance—keep a sharp look out.—There is many a happy slave.[20]

While the traditional arguments for marriage recognized its importance for the individual and the community, Leon and Amy Kass argue that our contemporary liberal and secular society, with its high premium on freedom and the pursuit of happiness, may need marriage even more than in the past. Marriage, they say, provides a brake against runaway individualism. While it is good for self-fulfillment, erotic satisfaction, or personal happiness, marriage also offers the possibilities for friendship: avoiding loneliness, expanding the self, and enjoying intense and deep intimacy.

Marriage and Children

As I was reflecting on the different arguments for and against marriage, one premise kept repeatedly to surface. Irrespective of its many problems, marriage continues to provide the best framework for organizing the life of individuals and of society. Marriage is the best framework to give human beings the long-term motivation and energy to strive and be productive, be grounded and connected, and rise above one's natural selfishness.

Marriage is also the best framework to socialize and humanize men, women, and children, and most importantly, it provides the prime environment for raising the next generation. It is the nucleus of a civilized society. Children born out of wedlock often substitute their need for family by banding together to form gangs and get their self-esteem from fast money, drugs, sex, and violence. If the majority of people would not marry and be responsible for their family, who or what would hold society together? There is a limit to how much a government can provide before a democracy loses its freedom.

While different forms of marriage have existed, monogamy is the best adapted to the task of rearing offspring in an advanced society. Two parents can do this job better than one. It is as though a species adopts monogamy "for the sake of the children," writes the sociologist William Tucker.[21] Moreover, according to Tucker, the most advanced and economically successful human civilizations are generally monogamous, because monogamy creates a social structure that reduces sexual competition among males, and enables the society to function as a cohesive whole. Societies that have been unable to establish monogamy have also been unable to create working democracies or widely distributed wealth.

Human beings are inherently free-spirited and amorphous social creatures. There is infinite number of conditions under which humans could live. There is a well of emotions, mostly dormant, ready to stir a person to action, at any given moment. Without formal marriage holding the social structure together, the fabric of society could soon unravel, rendering the culture increasingly chaotic, weak, and apathetic. It could then slowly inch toward a point of disintegration becoming easy prey for an authoritarian ruler or a more aggressive culture.

And so it can be summarized that the institution of marriage has two broad functions. It serves important needs of the individual—men, women, and children—and it also serves basic needs of society. All societies need children to be continuously born. Without a fresh yearly influx of new births, societies will atrophy, decline, and die. A nation's birthrate has to stand, at the minimum, at 2.1 children per woman to maintain replacement value, and be able to cover its costs. Healthy societies need healthy and well-developed children. There is ample evidence that children born and raised in two-parent families, and cared for by a parent in their early formative years, are developing the best. The future of America is clearly in the hands of responsible parents and parents-to-be who take their parenting role seriously; the more of them the better.

CHAPTER NINE

THE POWER OF LOVE

Love is the great intangible. The white light of emotions. It includes many feelings which we crowd into one simple word. And no one can agree on what it is . . . .

—Diane Ackerman, *A Natural History of Love*

What Is Love?

Let us now take a few moments to consider the topic of love. What is love? Does it exist in this day and age of widespread divorce? Is it important? And is it necessary for children's development? The poet Diane Ackerman describes love, in a charming book titled *A Natural History of Love*, as a powerful idea; an idea that can alter the flow of history. As she put it, love has inspired works of art, cheered the forlorn, turned tough guys to mush, consoled the enslaved, driven strong women mad, glorified the humble, fueled national scandals, bankrupted robber barons, and made mincemeat of kings.[1] Other people say that love is the most important thing in life, a passion for which we would fight or die. And still others claim that love is an intoxicant, a disease; a "stupidity of two," said Napoleon Bonaparte. And Francois de la Rochefoucauld declared: "There are people who would never have fallen in love if they never heard of it"

The concept is ancient; the passion is older than civilization. Any attempt to search for the source of the word "love" takes one vaguely back to the ancient Sanskrit word *lubhyati* ("he desires"). Thus much has been written about love throughout the ages, in all literate cultures, from earliest antiquity all the way to the present day.

The importance of the concept in human affairs is highlighted by the fact that "love" has more entries in John Bartlett's collection of *Familiar Quotations* than any other word—with Man, God, and

Death, listed second, third, and fourth after love. But what exactly is love? Why is it so difficult to define?

The Oxford Dictionary gives ten definitions to the noun and four definitions to the verb of love; from matters of the heart to the stuff of the heavens, from the bedroom, to the nursery, to the church, to the state. As historian Vern L. Bullough writes, "From the mother's caresses of a newborn infant to the sexual passion of two lovers, from the altruist's compassion for all humanity to the spurned lover's narrow hostility toward a former loved one."[2] George Chapman, the English poet, wrote: "I tell thee, love is nature's second sun causing a spring of virtue where he shines." It is "the glue of human existence," says Anthony Walsh, a professor of sociology. And Erich Fromm, the noted twentieth-century psychiatrist, concluded that love is the last hope for the problems of human existence.

A Psychiatrist's Point of View

More than fifty years ago, Fromm wrote a short volume titled *The Art of Loving*.[3] It was a best-seller for several decades (with over fifty printings) and it still is as fresh and thought provoking today. Fromm viewed love as an interpersonal union, the "fusion with another person." He considered it to be the answer to one of contemporary life's most basic existential problems: that is, the need to overcome one's feeling of separateness; as he put it, the need "To leave the prison of one's aloneness." According to Fromm, the desire for interpersonal fusion is the most powerful striving in man. It is the most fundamental passion; the force which keeps the human race together, the clan, the family, society. Failure to achieve this fusion means insanity or destruction—self destruction or destruction of others. Without love, humanity could not exist for a day, concluded Fromm.[4] He described the different kinds of love—romantic love, parents' love for their children, brotherly love, erotic love, self-love, and love of God—explaining that love is primarily about *giving*. It is about giving rather than receiving; giving of oneself rather than meting out material things. But while different kinds of love exist, said Fromm, certain basic elements are common to all forms of love, and these are *care, responsibility, respect,* and *knowledge.*

The problem is that contemporary men and women have only a limited capacity to truly love, observed Fromm. He argued that brotherly love, motherly love, and romantic love are relatively rare phenomena today, replaced by forms of pseudo-love. He was critical of Freud and his followers' overemphasis on sexuality, warning that "if we should not succeed in keeping alive a vision of mature life, then indeed we are confronted with the probability that our whole cultural tradition will break down."[5] Our tradition is not primarily based on the transmission of certain kinds of knowledge, but on the transmission of certain kinds of human traits, said Fromm. And if future generations will not see these traits, a five-thousand-year-old culture will break down, even if its knowledge is transmitted and further developed.

Love is the only sane and satisfactory answer to the problem of human existence, declared Fromm. "Any society which excludes the development of love must in the long run perish of its own contradiction with the basic necessities of human nature."[6] It is imperative, therefore, to learn what mature love means, advised Fromm, and to stop indulging in the images of pseudo-love portrayed in today's media,

Love and Young Children

So how does Fromm's theory relate to Young children? We discussed in earlier chapters children's existential need for their parents' love and attention. They need a stable nurturing relationship with their parents—in particular their mother, and especially in the early formative years to ensure optimal development. They need that love for optimal physical development, for optimal mental development, and especially, for their emotional and social development.

Parental attachment and love in the early formative years forms a template for a child's love ability as an adult. Early childhood experiences leave their imprint on a young child's brain. And early love experience will affect all future relationships of that child. As a child receives so will he or she be able to give. Let us then take a closer look at how love affects young children's development.

Love and Physical Development

Breastfeeding during the first year of life provides the most wholesome nutrition a baby can have, supplying the growing body with all the nutrients it needs for optimal development (see Chapter 4 for details). Breastfeeding is also the most basic process through which the mother/infant bond is established, enhancing the mother's maternal feelings toward her child, and wrapping the baby with a blanket of maternal bliss.

Loving tactile stimulation in the early years of life is now recognized to be especially important, because it reaches, through the nerve cells on the skin, the child's brain, and actually affects the infant's brain structure (by activating neurons and stimulating the growth of more synapses and dendrites.) Stimuli deprivation on the other hand, is known to lower neural metabolism and brain development (see Chapter 4 for more details).

Young children who are surrounded by a loving environment and receive adequate nutrition, shelter, clothing, protection, and a hygienic drug-free environment—including tactile and mental stimulation—have an overall enhanced health. Their home environment facilitates their optimal physical growth and the proper development of their nervous system. Under such conditions children thrive. On the other hand, when children lack a nurturing home environment and the loving support of their parents—when they suffer neglect—they develop a lower immune system and get sick more often. Physicians and psychiatrists have long recognized that love, or the lack of it, has a significant effect on both physical and mental illness of children from day one. .

The human infant is at the mercy of adults far longer than any other newborn. And the strong biologically based inclination on the part of the mother to care for her infant gives it the best chance to develop successfully through its period of dependency. "The human adult's willingness to invest time and energy in someone else's goals, even at the expense of one's own, is called love," writes Professor Walsh in *The Science of Love*.[7] We need to educate parents about the role of loving care and stimulation in the development of their child's body and personality, and encourage mothers to be with their infants as much as possible during the stage of neuronal growth, says Walsh.

Love and Mental Development

Consistent loving interaction affects also young children's mental development. A supportive home environment encourages communication and facilitates language acquisition and fluency. It stimulates awareness of the environment leading to questions and answers sessions, and thus the development of new concepts; it enhances memory skills, and promotes mental alertness and curiosity, encouraging creativity and problem- solving ability. The continuous stimulation that a supportive home environment provides, from an early age, activates synaptic formation and greater connectivity between brain cells, thus enriching and thickening the young child's brain, and increasing the brain's capacity and overall intelligence.

Most important, a child who feels loved is more open and eager (and therefore more able) to learn and absorb new information from the environment. That child's brain is not clouded by the toxic and numbing mix of negative feelings and emotions.

Love and Emotional/Social Development

There is a famous saying that since "God" cannot be everywhere, he invented mothers. According to Walsh, mothers are good for us because they make us happy, ease our anxiety; make us feel warm and secure, and "they keep our endorphins at pleasant levels, and make us 'high' on life."[8] This is all good.

But the greatest significance of a stable nurturing early parent-child relationship is for the child's social/emotional development. As discussed in chapter 3, regarding attachment, parental love encourages the development of children's self-identity, it promotes self-confidence and a sense of security, it can facilitate the development of self-control, empathy, and the ability to get along well with others, in addition to enhancing the child's general lovability.

Recent studies have found that family patterns that undermine nurturing care may lead to significant compromise in both cognitive and emotional capacities, while supportive, warm, nurturing emotional interactions with infants and young children help the central nervous system grow appropriately and develop positive thought and behavior patterns. When children have secure, empathetic, and nurturing relationships, they learn to be intimate and empathetic and eventually to communicate about their feelings, reflect on their own wishes, and develop their own relationships with peers and adults.[9]

"Show me a murderer, a hardened criminal, a juvenile delinquent, a psychopath, a 'cold fish' and in almost every case I will show you a tragedy that has resulted from not being properly loved during childhood," wrote Ashley Montagu, a renowned anthropologist.[10] And Walsh argues that the human infant can be molded and cultivated into a decent caring adult, or its development can be distorted horribly in a way that no nonhuman animal can be.[11]

Also the moral sense of right and wrong develops out of early emotional interactions. A child's ability to understand another person's feelings, and to care about how he or she feels, can arise only from the experiences that it has with nurturing interactions. We can feel empathy only if someone has been empathetic and caring with us. We cannot experience emotions that were never shown to us, and we cannot experience the consistency and intimacy of ongoing love unless we have had that experience with someone in our lives. At times it can be someone other than a parent, as, for example, a grandmother, an aunt, a nanny, or even a neighbor, but it must be there—stable, consistent, and supportive. A toddler who grows up feeling unloved will have difficulty showing love to others (in childhood or in adulthood). A youngster who has been abused will in all likelihood grow up to be an abuser.

The Role of Oxytocin

There has been a great deal of talk lately about oxytocin, better known as the "attachment hormone," or "the hormone of love", which is produced in women in high levels during childbirth and lactation. Oxytocin stimulates maternal behavior and affects the mother/infant bonding process. It reduces blood pressure, and the level of cortisol (the stress hormone), and anxiety. Oxytocin's level in a woman's bloodstream remains high as long as a mother breastfeeds her infant. Her hormonal system thus prepares her to be sensitively tuned to the needs of her infant. As long as the oxytocin's level is high it keeps the mother relaxed and less prone to be disturbed by environmental stressors, allowing for greater sensitivity to her infant. She can then give her child the care and stimulation that it needs for optimal development.

"In the critical task of humanizing the species, of teaching it to love, biologically and psychologically, nature has placed women at the center of the universe. No sexual politics are played here; anatomy may not be destiny, but modern neurophysiology is reaffirming Freud's belief of the centrality of the mother's role in making us human," writes Walsh.[12] And whether she is aware of it or not, the infant's mother is the major organizer of the child's brain during this critical period of exterogestation. "This is both her existential burden and her crowning glory," writes Walsh.

The Fruits of Love

A healthy sense of self is important today more than ever before. While not essential in America's agrarian past, when people were anchored in religious faith and extended family, it is essential today. Once economic independence became the expected norm, and higher education a necessary means to achieve that goal, people had to develop a better grasp of themselves. "Who am I?" "What do I want to do with my life?" "How am I going to support myself?" are common questions today. We no longer have family businesses to join; and where they do exist, adult children often do not want to follow in their parents' footsteps. A sense of self is, therefore, essential for blazing one's own course in life, but this needs to be developed. It can best evolve in a stable and nurturing home environment, where steadfast loving adult models exist for the children to observe, emulate, and reflect upon as they grow and develop.

A warm relationship between parents and children, and between mothers and fathers who are the primary model for their children, is important for raising human beings who are kind, empathic, helpful, thoughtful, resilient, productive, and strong. These qualities are the fruits of love. Love, of course, is not enough. Other ingredients, such as discipline, honesty and trust are also needed in the mix of a good environment. But as Fromm said, love is primary.

Love is the source of young children's energy and motivation to grow and develop. It is their glowing beacon. We rarely appreciate the immense effort it takes for youngsters to acquire their language—to learn the basic concepts of colors, shapes, and numbers; to understand the family unit, the days of the week, the calendar, in addition to learning the basic rules of behavior, and develop their physical skills. Yet children will strive and put the necessary effort into all that learning for the love of their parents. They will do their utmost to please the supportive adults around them, if these adults are only kind to them. But when they get frustrated for lack of love; when they are neglected, they will be less interested in their physical environment, grow increasingly apathetic, or become prone to burst into fits of rage and anger. Love is the invisible glue that holds a culture together, binding man to woman, parents to children, and individuals to a community, a nation.

The Warning of the Ik

I would like to end this chapter with a true story; a tragic horror story that can be read as a fable. A tale that describes what can happen to a people when all love is lost. It is the story of the Ik, as reported by the British-born anthropologist Colin Turnbull in his book titled *The Mountain People*, first published in 1972.[13]

The Ik are a small tribe of hunter-gatherers who live in a remote mountain region of northeastern Uganda. They were once prosperous. But when a new Ugandan government forbade them to hunt in a fertile part of their homeland, which was turned into a national park, the Ik were pushed into an arid region. After three generations that suffered through drought and starvation, the Ik people became hostile, selfish, and mean. They abandoned all values of trust, friendship, love, kindness, cooperation, family, the care of children, and respect for the life of other human beings. As Turnbull put it, they began to live beyond humanity. Individual survival was the only thing that mattered.

What was the nature of childcare in that deteriorating social environment? During the first three years of life, the Ik mother gave some minimal care to her children, but from then on, the children were expected to be on their own, and a series of *rites de passage* began. Children divided themselves into two age levels and formed age bands. The junior band consisted of children between the ages of three and seven; the senior age band included the eight- to twelve-year-olds. Entering a band, you are the youngest, have the least to offer, and are no asset to the group. But at least you will be in the band for four or five years, so it is known that if you survive, you will eventually be of some use.

Within the band each child seeks another child that is close to him or her in age, for defense against the older children. These become "friends." These friendships are temporary, however, and inevitably there comes a time, the time of transition, when each turns on the one that up to then has been the closest to him: that is the *rite de passage*, the destruction of that fragile bond called friendship. When this has happened to you three or four times, "you are ready for the world," wrote Turnbull.

Each morning the villagers—adults, children, and the old—left their compounds to scavenge for food; each person went by himself. The only fixed social groupings were the children's age bands, which moved as a whole. There were no fixed territories to forage, and if a senior band met a junior band and wished to take its territory, it did so by force—using fists, sticks or stones. Children gathered only as much food as they could eat. Hoarding was not tolerated. Since the younger children were too small and weak to climb up trees to reach the fruits, they were left with what they found on the ground—often figs that had been partially eaten by baboons. When they were terribly hungry and unable to find real food to eat, they swallowed dirt and pebbles. The weakest children soon died. The strongest survived to achieve the leadership position of the band, until he was driven out by a competing band member. In the senior band sexual interests begin to appear providing an alternative way to win friends. Even eight-year-old girls soon learned that their body was useful.

After two years of life among the Ik, Turnbull traveled back to civilization, returning a year later for a visit. It had been a rainy year, producing many plants. But despite the abundance of crops found rotting in the fields the Ik had not changed. Lovelessness had taken root in the Ik culture, Turnbull concluded, and it was spreading like a wild weed. The family no longer mattered—neither emotionally nor economically. Neither did friendship, or respect for life. The population was quickly dwindling.

What can we learn from the sad story of the Ik? Are there any parallels in Western society? I leave it to you to decide. There is no doubt that love can provide a cushion from the harshness of the world, making it a friendlier and a more livable place. The Ik also show us how human beings may look when their capacity for love is lost; and their raw nerves are exposed. It behooves us to reflect on this tragic story, and see in it a warning.

CHAPTER TEN

WHAT IS YOUR PURPOSE IN LIFE?

Without a purpose, life is motion without meaning, activity without direction, and events without reason. Without a purpose, life is trivial, petty, and pointless.

–Rick Warren, *The Purpose Driven Life*

One Needs a Purpose in Life

This last chapter could have actually been the first chapter of this book raising an existential question such as "what is your purpose in life?" Thomas Carlyle, the Scottish essayist and historian, is quoted as saying many years ago that "the man without a purpose is like a ship without a rudder." George Bernard Shaw, reflecting on the same topic, wrote: "This is the true joy of life: the being used up for a purpose recognized by yourself as a mighty one . . . being a force of nature instead of a feverish, selfish little clot of ailments and grievances, complaining that the world will not devote itself to making you happy "(*Man and Superman*). And Pastor Rick Warren, *New York Times* #1 best-selling author, wrote: "Knowing your purpose simplifies your life. It defines what you do and what you don't do; your purpose becomes the standard you use to evaluate which activities are essential and which aren't."[1]

So if a purposeful life is necessary to having a good and meaningful life, what is your life's purpose? Each person is driven by something. What drives you? According to Warren there are five common driving forces:

Common Driving Forces

1. Many people are driven by guilt. These people spend their entire lives running from regrets and hiding their shame. "They allow their past to control their future."

2. People are often driven by resentment. They hold on to hurts and never get over them.

3. Some people are driven by fear. Their fear may be the result of some traumatic experience, unrealistic expectations, poor upbringing, or even some genetic predisposition. Regardless of the cause, these people often miss good opportunities, being fearful to even try.

4. People are often driven by materialism. While achieving financial security is a positive goal, these people believe that having more of this or of that will make them happier, more important, and more secure.

5. Many people are driven by the need for approval. They allow the expectations of their parents, spouses, children, or friends to control their lives.

Love and Competition

To this list of Warren's driving forces I would like to add two more that merit highlighting; two additional driving forces that often conflict in today's life, creating a problem for many people. I am thinking of love and competition. "Love is the most powerful and still the most unknown energy of the world," said the French philosopher Pierre Teilhard de Chardin.[2] Erich Fromm, as we saw in the previous chapter, considered love to be "the most powerful striving in man," a necessary passion to "keep the human race together." So if love is recognized to be a powerful and necessary energy for which all people strive, it ought to be considered another driving force that motivates and moves our lives.

Now competition is another common driving force. The dictionary defines competition as the rivalry for supremacy or a prize; the struggle among organisms, for food, space, and other vital requirements. Competition has been a primary driving force in the evolutionary struggle. It has always been part of the human experience. Unfortunately, when competition is out of control, manifesting at the wrong place and at the wrong time, it can ruin lives.

Consider how the desire for love can be problematic for a highly competitive individual who may lack the maturity, patience, or will to nurture his or her love relationship, or defer it to when he or she is able to spend the necessary time to nurture it. Without nurture, feelings of love may get frustrated, dry out, and end in resentment and anger.

The potential conflict between love and competition is especially poignant today—causing serious relationship difficulties between men and women. Throughout history, women were either subservient to men or cooperative with them but they were never seriously competing with men. Yet since the 1970s, many women have started to compete with men in all spheres of life—from the bedroom to the boardroom, from the kitchen to the military, the church, and the university–often changing the age—old dynamic between the two genders, and affecting the most basic of human behavior. This includes the way we raise our children.

While the competitive drive may be desirable in one's professional life, it can be disastrous in one's personal life. If a couple in an intimate relationship, in marriage or outside marriage, is seriously competing with each other, their relationship will be difficult. It will lack harmony. That couple will have difficulty to develop a truly mature loving relationship. And they will be less likely to provide a good nurturing environment, and a positive example, for their young developing children.

Mature Love

Mature love is about giving, not only taking; thinking about the good of the other, not just about the self. Competition, on the other hand, is about the display of the self. If both the man and the woman in an intimate relationship are seriously competing with each other, they will be less likely to give. Their competitiveness may undermine their love and possibly be destructive for their marriage and their children's development. It may also sap their natural desire to have children, weakening their inherent instinct of survival.

Each of these driving forces—be it guilt, resentment, materialism, fear, the need for approval, or competition and love—can motivate a person to act. Each of these drives can energize, keep a person busy, and help secure a living, or provide a focus for one's life—for a while. But none of these driving forces will provide a lasting fulfillment, and give full meaning to one's life, without a clearly defined overall purpose. Without a long-term meaningful goal, these driving forces will at the end of the day leave one feeling empty, and searching.

What is Your Purpose?

Once we understand the forces that drive us, we can go back to our starting question of **what is your purpose in life.** If you have a religious orientation to life and the Bible is important to you, the answer may be relatively simple. "Be fruitful and multiply, fill the earth and subdue it; and rule over the fish of the sea, the bird of the sky, and every living thing that moves on the earth," were among God's first commandments to Adam and Eve (Genesis 1:28). In Genesis 2:15, we are told that "God took the man and placed him in the Garden of Eden, to work it and to guard it." In other words, the purpose of mankind, according to the Bible, is to procreate and take care of the world and all life that exists on it.

But if you are a responsible secular person, your purpose in life may surprisingly turn out to be not very different from the biblical commands discussed above. Many secularists are involved to some degree with an array of environmental issues—which is just another term for taking care of the world. Secularists are also concerned about issues involving the human condition, including human rights, universal healthcare, gun control, and so forth.

As for the biblical command to procreate—an order much more closely observed by the religiously oriented—secular America may soon find itself rethinking its attitude. An attitudinal resetting is increasingly likely to occur turning also secularists to be more in line with the biblical command discussed above.

Consider. As discussed in previous chapters, the twentieth century saw a sharp decline in the American birthrate. Significant numbers of women (white middle class women in particular) have been postponing motherhood until it is often too late for them to conceive. Other women are giving up motherhood altogether in favor of a rewarding career or a higher standard of living. And practically most women are sharply limiting the number of their children, as compared with past practice. The end result of this new attitude toward motherhood is a worrisome demographic projection.

Falling birthrates are accompanied by a rapidly aging population, and a shortage of people needed to fill the requirements of the job market, and to meet the expenses of Social Security, pensions, Medicare, Medicaid, education, and the military. New job creation also declines in an aging population, sharply affecting the nation's economy. The current economic problems and high unemployment are most likely temporary and the economy will rebound once new policies are introduced that will free the American people to pursue their initiatives and control of their lives.

There is no way America can remain a vibrant nation without raising its birthrate, to reach at least replacement level. Once this is realized, and the public becomes aware of the problem and its implications, it is likely to awaken the national instinct of survival and persuade also secularists to start having more kids. "There is a need to concentrate on the human factors," says Longman, to assure adequate fertility rates, strong families, lifelong education, and a more productive aging. These are the important raw materials that will secure American progress and prosperity in the future, he says.

Procreation or Immigration

A reliance on immigration to solve America's demographic problem, as has been the case in Western European nations, would be national suicide. America is a unique country, still the envy of the world, with particular national characteristics. Yes, it is a country that has always welcomed immigration and will no doubt continue to do so. And it would be easy to open the borders and let many more millions come in. However, it is important to emphasize that the influx of new immigrants into the United States was always controlled, and maintaining a healthy balance between the native-born American population and newcomers, in order to preserve the unique American characteristics, culture, and national identity.

Moreover, many immigrants today, unlike immigrants in past generations, refuse to integrate into mainstream American culture. Many want to benefit from the American experience, but continue to maintain their separate customs, traditions, culture, and even laws, of their country of origin. It is therefore, important for America to learn from the recent European experience. Realize that European nations that have sharply lowered their birthrate while letting floods of immigrants come into their country do the necessary work are now considered by demographers and political observers to be culturally dying. Large sections of major European cities do not have any more the appearance or the cultural characteristics of their unique past heritage, to the chagrin of these countries authorities and their public at large. We have to protect the United States from such a possibility.

Conclusion

In conclusion, one can say that the purpose of life is to continue and advance the human experience to its highest possible level. This requires first of all a healthy fertility rate, reaching at least replacement level of 2.1 children per woman. Yet giving birth to more children, by itself, will not be enough. Third world nations have a high birthrate and yet they remain underdeveloped. Greater attention must also be given to how we raise the kids; the kind of environment we create for them; the type of care we provide; and the educational goals that we formulate. This effort will require a stable and responsible home environment that includes a mother and a father who can work together in harmony and cooperation. Nothing is more essential to the future of a nation than a vibrant and healthy younger generation. No purpose in life is more simple and basic than that.

All human pursuits exist in order to serve and improve the human condition. Be it medicine, education, food production, science and technology, the arts, the military, the law, and so on, are all meant to serve and improve life. But all human pursuits are secondary to, and based on, the primary purpose of creating and maintaining life, and helping develop it to its highest possible potential. The future of America depends, therefore, not only on the size of its population but also on the quality of its people: their physical health, their mental health, their socio-emotional strength and stability, and their talent and creativity. We have the knowledge today how best to encourage our children's development in all these areas.

As to who should create life in a culture in which many women postpone motherhood or give it up altogether, it seems only fair that those who were given the gift of life should give life in return (once they are able and willing to provide for it) to help continue the life process of this nation. The growth and health of a democratic society must be the responsibility of its healthy adult majority, to ensure a robust national gene pool, and a continuation of the democratic process.

A good education is indispensable today to securing financial independence. Financial independence is necessary in order to obtain the basic necessities for a quality life, and to create a good environment for young developing children. A meaningful profession will enhance life's purpose. Some types of work will be essential to sustain and protect life; others will help make life more interesting and enjoyable. Still others will provide some fun for relaxation and emotional well-being. But all occupations are based on the first and most fundamental need of creating life and developing it to a healthy productive adulthood. "You were put on earth to make a contribution," said Rick Warren. It is your challenge to figure out what will be your contribution to life, and what is your purpose.

While *The Drama of the Mother-Child Bond* was in production, an interesting national debate erupted following the publication of an article by Anne-Marie Slaughter in the Atlantic of July/August 2012. Titled *Why Women Still Can't Have it all,* this article addresses the motherhood/career dilemma of a highly successful woman and her decision to drop out of a "dream" career in Washington in order to be home with her husband and two teen age sons (and continue "only" her tenured position as a professor at Princeton University.) This article, and the hot debate that followed, highlight the timeliness of *The Drama of the Mother-Child Bond.* I hope that my book will help clarify the very issues involved.

Dr. Ada Anbar
July 8, 2012.

Notes

CHAPTER 1: MOTHERHOOD, CAREER, AND CHILDREN

1. Sarah Baldauf, *U.S. & World Report*, February (2010), 24-26. David Shenk. *The Genius in All of Us.* (New York: Doubleday, 2010).
2. Lia Macko and Kerry Rubin, *Midlife Crisis at 30*, (Rodale, 2004), 15.
3. Maureen Dowd, *Are Men Necessary?* (New York: G.P. Putnam's Sons, 2005).

CHAPTER 2: SIX REASONS TO HAVE CHILDREN

1. Genesis, 30:1.
2. Genesis, 1:28.
3. Daphne de Marneffe, *Maternal Desire.* New York: Little, Brown and Company, (2004), 9.
4. Ibid, (from the book jacket).
5. Amy and Leon Kass, *Wing to Wing Oar to Oar*, (University of Notre Dame Press), 17.
6. Ibid, 25.
7. Ann Daly, *Inventing Motherhood*, (New York: Schocken Books, 1982), 18-19.
8. Maureen Dowd, *Are Men Necessary?* (New York: G.P. Putnam's Sons, 2005, 234.
9. Mike Stobbe, "37 Percent of U.S. Birth Out of Wedlock" *Associated Press*, November 21, (2006).
10. CDC, Center for Disease Control and Prevention, *U.S. Department of Health and Human Services*, "National Vital Statistics Reports, " Dec 5 (2007) Vol. 56, No.
11. Heather MacDonald, "Hispanic Family Values?" in *City Journal*, Autumn (2006).

12. Peggy Schulze., "Hispanic Family Values?" *City Journal, Autumn,* (2006).
13. Amanda Gan, "Hispanic Family Values?" *City Journal, Autumn* (2006).
14. Amy Braun, "Hispanic Family Values?" *City Journal,* Autumn (2006).
15. T. Berry Brazelton, *Touchpoints Birth to Three,* 2nd ed. (Cambridge, MA: De Capo Press, 2006).
16. Maureen Dowd, *Are Men Necessary?* (New York: G.P. Putnam's Sons, 1964), 64-65.
17. Lia Macko and Kerry Rubin, *Midlife Crisis at 30.* (New York: Rodale, 2004), 10.
18. Ibid., 12.
19. Leslie Morgan Steiner, *Mommy Wars,* (New York: Random House, 2006), 331.

CHAPTER 3: THE BONDING YEARS

1. John Bowlby, *Attachmebnt and Loss* (London: Hogarth Press, 1971).
2. Ibid., *A Secure Base* (New York: Basic Books, 1988), 1-2.
3. Jay Belsky, in *Becoming Attached,* Robert Karen, (New York: Oxford University Press, 1994), 7-8.
4. Robert Karen, *Becoming* Attached (New York: Oxford University Press, 1994), 340.
5. Ibid., 441.
6. Ken Magid, *High Risk, Children without a Conscience* (1987), ix-x.
7. Lawrence Hedges, *In Search of the Lost Mother of Infancy* (Jason Aronson, Inc., 1994), 3.
8. Ibid., 4.
9. Ibid, 5.
10. Kate O'Beirne, *Women Who Make the World Worse* (New York: Sentinel), 34.

11. Sandra Scarr, *Mother Care Other Care* (Penguin Books, 1984), from the book's jacket.

12. Ibid., as reported by Kate O'Beirne in *Women Who Make the World Worse* (New York: Sentinel), 40.

13. Robert Karen, *Becoming Attached* (New York: Oxford University Press, 1994), 343.

14. William and Wendy Dreskin, *The Day Care Decision* (New York: M. Evans & Co. 1983), 11.

15. Kate O'Beime, *Women Who Make the World Worse* (New York: Sentinel), 35.

16. Bernard Goldberg, as reported by Kate O'Beirne in *Women Who Make the World Worse* (New York: Sentinel), 36.

17. Shari L. Thurer, *The Myths of Motherhood* (New York: Penguin Books, 1994), xi.

18. Ibid., 278.

19. Ibid., xv.

20. Kate O'Beirne, *Women Who Make the World Worse* (New York: Sentinel), 35.

21. John Bowlby, as reported by Robert Karen in *Becoming Attached* (New York: Oxford University Press, 1994), 338.

22. T. Berry Brazelton and Stanley I. Greenspan, *The Irreducible Needs of Children* (Cambridge MA: Perseus Publ, 2000), 2.

23. Stanley I. Greenspan, *The Four Thirds Solution* (Cambridge, MA: Perseus Publishing, 2001), 5.

24. Ibid., 10.

25. Ibid., 92-93.

26. Ibid., 234.

27. Joan Peters, *Not Your Mother's Life* (Cambridge, MA: Persus Books, 2001), xii.

28. Ann Crittenden, *The Price of Motherhood* (New York: Metropolitan Books, 2001), 1.

29. Ibid., 37

30. Ibid., 39.

31. Ibid., 43.
32. Ibid., 105.
33. Sylvia Ann Hewlett, *Creating a Life*, (New York: Talk Miramax Books, 2002), 5.
34. Ibid., 114.
35. Ibid., 215.
36. Daphne de Marneffe, *Maternal Desire* (New York: Little Brown and Company, 2004), 159.
37. Ibid., vii.
38. Ibid., viii-x.
39. Ibid., from the book's jacket.
40. Susan J. Douglas and Meredith W. Michaels, The Mommy Myth (New York: Free Press, 2004), 237-238.
41. Ibid., 27.
42. Ibid., 299.
43. Ibid., 27.
44. Ibid., 27
45. William Sears and Martha Sears, *The Attachment Parenting Book* (New York: Little Brown and Company, 2001).
46. Mary Ainsworth, in an interview with Robert Karen, in *Becoming Attached* (New York: Oxford Univ. Press, 1994), 339.

CHAPTER 4: MOTHERHOOD TODAY

1. Shari L. Thurer, *The Myths of Motherhood* (New York: Penguin Books, 1994), 4.
2. Ann Dally, Inventing Motherhood (New York: Schocken Books, 1982), 17.
3. Ibid., 21.
4. Daphne de Marneffe, *Maternal Desire* (New York: Little, Brown and Company, 2004), 160.
5. Craig A. Cooney, "Nutrients, epigenetics, and embryonic development" in *Nutriets and Epigenetics*, Boca Raton, FL:CRC Press, (2009): 155-169.

6. Lise Eliot, *What's Going On in There?* (New York: Bantam Books, 1999), 240.
7. Stanley I. Greenspan, *The Irreducible Needs of Children* (Cambridge, MA: Perseus Publishing, 2000), 60.
8. T. Berry Brazelton and Stanley I. Greenspan, *The Irreducible Needs of Children* (Cambridge, MA: Perseus Publ., 2000), 74.
9. Daphne de Marneffe, *Maternal Desire* (New York: Little, Brown and Company, 2004), 20.
10. Ibid., 22.
11. Susan J. Douglas and Meredith W. Michaels, *The Mommy Myth* (New York: Free Press, 2004), 299.
12. Daphne de Marneffe, *Maternal Desire* (New York: Little, Brown and Company, 2004), 22.
13. Stanley Greenspan, *The Four Thirds Solution* (Cambridge, MA: Perseus Publishing, 2001), 85.
14. David Satcher, U.S. Department of Health and Human Services, (*HHS Blueprint for Action on Breastfeeding*), Washington D.C. (2000), 3.
15. Lise Eliot, *What's Going On in There?* (New York: Little, Brown and Company), 184.
16. James W. Anderson, Bryan M. Johnstone and Daniel T. Remley, "Breast-feeding and cognitive development: a meta-analysis. *American Journal of Clinical Nutrition, Vol 70, No 4, 525-535, Oct. 1999.*
17. Office on Women's Health, Department of Health and Human Services, "*Breastfeeding–HHS Blueprint for Action on Breastfeeding,* "Washington, D.C. (2000), 1-33.
18. William Sears and Martha Sears, *The Attachment Parenting Book* (New York: Little, Brown and Company, 2001), 14.
19. Gale Pryor, *Nursing Mother; Working mother: The essential guide for breastfeeding and staying close to your baby after you return to work.*http://pregnancyandbaby.com/Building-a-relationship-471.htm.

20. Ibid.
21. Lise Eliot, *What's Going On in There?* (New York: Bantam Books, 1999), 23.
22. Ibid., 27.
23. Ibid., 32.
24. T. Berry Brazelton and Stanley I. Greenspan, *The Irreducible Needs of Children* (Cambridge, MA: Perseus Publishing, 2000), 2.
25. Ibid., xi.
26. Ann Dally, *Inventing Motherhood*, (New York: Schocken Books, 1982), 191.
27. Lise Eliot, *What's Going On in There?* (New York: Bantam Books, 1999), 306.
28. Ray Kurzweil, *The Singularity is Near* (London: Penguin Books, 2006), 193.
29. T. Berry Brazelton and Stanley I. Greenspan, *The Irreducible Needs of Children* (Cambridge, MA: Perseus Publishing, 2000), 4.
30. Lise Eliot, *What's Going On in There?* (New York: Bantam Books, 1999), 305.
31. Stanley I. Greenspan, *The Four Thirds Solution* (Cambridge, MA: Perseus Publishing, 2001), 133.
32. Ibid.
33. Lise Eliot, *What's Going On in There?* (New York: Bantam Books, 1999), 349.
34. Ibid., 350.
35. Ibid., 354.
36. Benjamin S. Bloom, *Stability and Change in Human Characteristics* (New York: John Wiley & Sons, 1964), 68.
37. Lise Eliot, *What's Going On in There?* (New York: Bantam Books, 1999), 427.
38. Pia Rebello Britto, Jeanne Brooks-Gunn, and Terri M. Griffin, "Maternal Reading and Teaching Patterns: Associations with School Readiness in Low-Income African American Families" in *RRQ*, Vol 41, 1, (2006), 68-86.

39. T. Berry Brazelton and Stanley I. Greenspan, *The Irreducible Needs of Children"* (Cambridge, MA: Perseus Publishing, 2000), 146.
40. Ada Anbar, *How to Choose a Nursery School* (Palo Alto, CA, Pacific Books, Publishers, 1999).
41. Lise Eliot, *What's Going On in There?* (New York: Bantam Books, 1999), 459-460.
42. Ibid., 460.
43. Ibid.., 460.
44. Daphne de Marneffe, *Maternal Desire* (New York: Little, Brown and Company, 2004), 20.

CHAPTER 5: DAYCARE'S ILLUSION

1. T. Berry Brazelton and Stenley I. Greenspan, *The Irreducible Needs of Children* (Cambridge, MA: Perseus Publishing, 2000), 12.
2. Ibid., 24.
3. Ibid., 26.
4. Ibid., 8.
5. Susan J. Douglas and Meredith W. Michaels, The *Mommy Myth* (New York: Free Press, 2004), 238.
6. Swedish Information Service, 2009 www.sweden.se.
7. Organiztion for Economic Cooperation and Development, http://www.oecd.
8. NICHD Early Child Care Research Network (edited), *Child Care and Child Development* (NewYork: The Guilford Pr., 2005), 435.
9. Kathleen Kieman, "European Perspective on Nonmarital Childbearing." In *Out of Wedlock*, eds. Lawrence L. Wu and Barbara Wolfe (New York: Russell Sage Foundation, 2001), 77-108.
10. NICHD Early Child Care Research Network (edited), *Child Care and Child Development* (New York: The Guilford Press, 2005).
11. Ibid., 430.

12. Ibid., 174.
13. Ibid., 48.
14. Ibid., 66.
15. Alison Clarke-Stewart and Virginia D. Allhusen, *What We Know About Childcare* (Cambridge, MA: Harvard University Press, 2005), 90.
16. Ibid.
17. NICHD Early Child Care Research Network (edited), *Child Care and Child Development* (New York: The Guilford Press, 2005), 315.
18. Ibid., 192.
19. Ibid., 391.
20. Ibid., 435.
21. Ibid., 435.
22. Richard Garner, "British parents spend least time with children." *The Independent & The Independent on Sunday*, 5 April, (2007).
23. Kate O'Beirne, *Women Who Make the World Worse* (New York: Sentinel, 2006), 37.
24. Ibid., 23.
25. Ibid., 30.
26. Ibid., 40.
27. U.S. Department of Commerce, *Household Economic Studies* "Who's Minding the Kids? Child Care Arrangements: Winter 2002, (October 2005).
28. Kate O'Beirne, *Women Who Make the World Worse* (New York: Sentinel, 2996), xviii.

CHAPTER 6: SHOULD EVERY WOMAN BECOME A MOTHER?

1. Inda Schaenen, in *Mommy Wars* by Leslie Morgan Steiner (New York: Random House, 2006), 239.
2. Ann Dally, *Inventing Motherhood*, (New York: Schocken Books, 1982), 189.

3. Daphne de Marneffe, *Maternal Desire* (New York: Little, Brown and Company, 2004), 216.
4. Ann Dally, *Inventing Motherhood* (New York: Schocken Books, 1982), 18.
5. Amy and Leon Kass, *Wing to Wing, Oar to Oar* (University of Notre Dam Press, 1999), 25.
6. Phillip Longman, *The Empty Cradle* (New York: New America Books, 2004), 15.
7. Germaine Greer, *The Female Eunuch*, quoted in *Inventing Motherhood*, by Ann Dally (New York: Schocken Books, 1982), 174.
8. Ann Dally, *Inventing Motherhood* (New York: Schocken Books, 1982), 173.
9. Judith Warner, *Perfect Madness* (New York: Riverhead Books, 2005), 54.
10. Maria Martinelli, quoted by William and Wendy Dreskin, in *The Day Care Decision* (1983), (New York: M. Evans & Co.) 106.
11. Maureen Dowd, *Are Men Necessary?* (New York: G.P. Putnam's Sons, 2005), 8.
12. Judith Warner, *Perfect Madness* (New York: Riverhead Books, 2005), 46.
13. Ann Dally, *Inventing Motherhood* (New York: Schocken Books, 1982), 18-19.
14. Maureen Dowd, *Are Men Necessary?* (New York: G.P. Putnam's Sons, 2005), 234.
15. Leslie Morgan Steiner, *Mommy Wars* (New York: Random House, 2006), 330.
16. Phillip Longman, *The Empty Cradle* (New York: New America Books, 2004), 16.
17. Ibid., 17.
18. Ibid., 18.
19. Ann Dally, *Inventing Motherhood* (New York: Schocken Books, 1982), 17.

20. Ibid., 318.
21. Sylvia Ann, Hewlett, *Creating a Life* (New York: Talk Miramax Books, 2002), 216.
22. Ibid., 205.
23. Ibid., 215.
24. Mary Ann Mason and Eve Mason Ekman, *Mothers on the Fast Track* (New York: Oxford University Press, 2007), 123.
25. Bernadine Healy, "The Cry of the Children," *U.S. News & World Report*, September 3, (2007), 82.
26. Wendy Mogel, *The Blessing of a Skinned Knee* (New York: Scribner, 2001), 22.
27. Ann Dally, *Inventing Motherhood* (New York: Schocken Books, 1982), 323.
28. Mary Ann Mason and Eve Mason Ekman, *Mothers on the Fast Track* (New York: Oxford University Press, 2007), 48.

CHAPTER 7: A NEW PARADIGM FOR AMERICAN MOTHERHOOD

1. Madelein Albright, www.answers.com/topic/madelein-albright.
2. Wendy Sachs, *How She Really Does It* (Cambridge, MA: De Capo Press, 2005), 180.
3. Nita Lowey, (http://lowey.house.gov/index.cfm).
4. SandraD. O'Connor(http://phoenix.about.com/cs/famous/a/oconnor.htm).
5. Ann Dally, *Inventing Motherhood* (New York: Schocken Books, 1982), 324.

CHAPTER 8: IS MARRIAGE NECESSARY?

1. Robert L. Griswold, "Divorce Rates" in *Divorce Statistics Collection* (2006), 9. WWW. Divorcereform.org/rates.html
2. Census Bureau Statistics, www.divorcereform.org/rates.html (2006), 3.

3. Mike Stobbe, "37 Percent of U.S. Births Out of Wedlock," *Associated Press*, (November 21, 2006).
4. Clarence Page, "Out-of-Wedlock Births in Black America," Interview on *NPR* (September 27, 2005).
5. Heather MacDonald, "Hispanic Family Values? *City Journal (Autumn* 2006).
6. Herbert S. Klein, *A Population History of the United States* (Cambridge University Press, 2004).
7. Sanders Korenman, Robert Kaestner, and Theodore J. Joyce, "Unintended Pregnancy and the Consequences of Nonmarital Childbearing." In *Out of Wedlock,* eds. Lawrence L. Wu and Barbara Wolfe (New York: Russell Sage Foundation, 2001), 259-286.
8. Amy and Leon Kass, *Wing to Wing, Oar to Oar* (University of Notre Dame Press, 1999), 81.
9. Maureen Dowd, *Are Men Necessary?* (New York: G.P. Putnam's Sons , 2005), 42.
10. Ibid., 52.
11. Ibid., 52.
12. Lia Macko and Kerry Rubin, *Midlife Crisis at 30* (New York: Rodale Books, 2004), 15.
13. Daniel Levinson, quoted by Lia Macko and Kerry Rubin, in *Midlife Crisis at 30* (New York: Rodale Books, 2004), 12.
14. Lia Macko and Kerry Rubin, *Midlife Crisis at 30* (New York: Rodale Books, 2004), 35.
15. Ibid., 10.
16. Editorial, *Women Today,* July 27, 2011.
17. Maureen Dowd, *Are Men Necessary?* (New York: G.P. Putnam's Sons, 2005), 62.
18. Ibid., 65.
19. Charles Darwin, in *Wing to Wing, Oar to Oar,* by Amy and Leon Kass, (University of Notre Dame Press, 1999), 84.
20. Ibid., 85.

21. William Tucker, in *Wing to Wing, Oar to Oar,* by Amy and Leon Kass University of Notre Dame Press, 1999), 129.

CHAPTER 9: THE POWER OF LOVE

1. Diane Ackerman, *A Natural History of Love* (New York: Vintage Books, 1995).
2. Vern L. Bullough, in *The Science of Love,* by Anthony Walsh (Buffalo, NY: Prometheus Books, 1996), 6.
3. Erich Fromm, *The Art of Loving* (New York: Bantam Books, 1956).
4. Ibid., 15.
5. Ibid., 99.
6. Ibid., 112.
7. Anthony Walsh, *The Science of Love* (Buffalo, NY: Prometheus Books, 1996), 42.
8. Ibid., 41.
9. T. Berry Brazelton and Stanley I. Greenspan, *The Irreducible Needs of Children* (Cambridge, MA: Perseus Publishing, 2000), 3.
10. Ashley Montagu, in *A Natural History of Love* by Diane Ackerman (New York: Vintage Books, 1995), 148.
11. Anthony Walsh, *The Science of Love* (Buffalo, NY: Prometheus Books, 1996), 44.
12. Ibid., 37.
13. Colin Turnbull, *The Mountain People* (New York: Touchstone, 1972).

CHAPTER 10: WHAT IS YOUR PURPOSE IN LIFE?

1. Rick Warren, *The Purpose Driven Life* (Grand Rapids, MI: Zondervan, 2007), 31.
2. Pierre Teilhard de Chardin, in *Mothers,* by Alexandra Stoddard (New York: William Morrow and Company, 1996), 95.

Selected Bibliography

Ackerman, Diane. *A Natural History of Love*. New York: Vintage Books, 1995.

American College of Obstetricians and Gynecologists, *Patient Education Pamphlet*, 2000, Washington, DC.

Baldauf, Sarah, *U.S. News & World Report*, February (2010): 24-26.

Bowlby, J. *A Secure Base*. New York: Basic Books, 1988.

Belsky Jay, "Interactional and Contextual Determinants of Attachment Security" in Handbook of Attachment, ed. Jude Cassidy and Phillip R. Shaver, 249—264. New York: The Guilford Press, 1999.

Bloom, S. Benjamin. *Stability and Change in Human Characteristics*. New York: John Wiley & Sons, 1964.

Brazelton, Berry T. and Stanley I. Greenspan. *The Irreducible Needs of Children,*. Cambridge, Ma: Perseus Publishing, 2000.

Brazelton, T. Berry. *Touchpoints Birth to Three*, 2nd ed. Cambridge, MA: Da Capo Press, 2006.

Bullough, Vern L. in *The Science of Love,* by Anthony Walsh. Buffalo New York, Prometheus, 1996.

Cassidy, Jude and Phillip R. Shaver, Eds., *Handbook of Attachment*, New York: The Guilford Press, 1999.

Cassidy Jude, "The Nature of the Child's Ties" in *Handbook of Attachment*, eds. Jude Cassidy and Phillip R. Shaver, 3-20. New York: The Guilford Press, 1999.

Clarke-Stewart, Alison. and Virginia D. Allhusen. *What we Know about Childcare*. Cambridge, Massachusetts: Harvard University Press, 2005.

Clarkson, Sally. *The Mission of Motherhood*, Colorado Springs, Colorado: WaterBrook Press, 2003.

Cooney, Craig A. "Nutrients, epigenetics, and embryonic development" in *Nutrients and Epigenetics*, Boca Raton, Fl.: CRC Press, (2009): 155-169.

Crittenden Ann, *The Price of Motherhood*, New York: Metropolitan Books, 2001.

Dally, Ann, *Inventing Motherhood*, New York: Schocken Books, 1982.

Dreskin, William and Wendy, *The Day Care Decision*, New York: M. Evans & Co. 1983.

Douglas, Susan J. and Meredith W. Michaels. *The Mommy Myth*. New York: Free Press, 2004.

Dowd, Maureen, *Are Men Necessary?* New York: G.P. Putnam's Sons, 2005.

Eliot, Lise. *What's Going on in There?* New York: Bantam Books, 1999.

Fromm, Erich. *The Art of Loving*, New York: Bantam Book, 1956.

Garner, Richard. "British parents spend least time with children." *The Independent & The Independent on Sunday*, 5 April, 2007. Independent Online Edition

Goodman, Michelle. *The Anti 9-To-5 Guide*, Emeryvill, CA: Seal Press, 2007.

Greenspan, Stanley I.. *The Growth of the Mind.* Addison-Wesley Publishing Complany, Inc. 1997.

Granju, Katie Allison, with Betsy Kennedy, R.N.. M.S.N. *Attachment Parenting.* New York: Pocket Books, 1999.

Greenspan, Stanley I. *The Four Thirds Solution.* Cambridge, MA: Perseus Publishing, 2001.

Greenspan, Stanley I., *Great Kids.* Cambridge, MA: Da Capo Press, 2007.

Griswold, L. Robert. *Divorce Statistics Collection.* WWW. Divorcereform.org/rates.html p. 9, 2006.

Grossmann, Klaus E., Grossmann Karin, and Everett Waters eds. *Attachment from Infancy to Adulthood.* New York: The Guilford Press, 2005.

Hantrais, Linda. "Living as a Family in Europe" presented at the European Population Conference 2005, Strasbourg, 7-8 April 2005.

Bernadine Healy, M.D. "The Cry of the Children", *U.S. News & World Report*, September 3, (2007), 82.

Hewlett, Sylvia Ann. *Creating a Life: Professional Women and the Quest for Children.* New York: Talk Miramax Books, 2002.

Karen, Robert. *Becoming Attached*. New York: Warner Books Inc. 1994.

Kass, Amy and Leon, *Wing to Wing, Oar to Oar,* University of Notre Dame Press, 1999.

Kiernan, Kathleen. "European Perspectives on Nonmarital Childbearing." In *Out of Wedlock*, eds. Lawrence L. Wu and Barbara Wolfe, 77-108. New York: Russell Sage Foundation, 2001.

Klein, S. Herbert. *A Population History of the United States,* Cambridge University Press, 2004.

Korenman, Sanders, Robert Kaestner, and Theodore J. Joyce. "Unintended Pregnancy and the Consequences of Nonmarital Childbearing." In *Out of Wedlock*, eds. Lawrence L. Wu and Barbara Wolfe, 259-286. New York: Russell Sage Foundation, 2001.

Kurzweil, Ray, *The Singularity is Near*, London: Penguin Books, 2006.

La Leche League International, *The Womanly Art of Breastfeeding.* New York: A Plume Book, 2004.

Longman Phillip, *The Empty Cradle.* New York: New America Books, 2004.

Lukas L. Carrie. *Women, Sex, and Feminism.* Washington, DC. : Regnery Publishing, Inc., 2006.

MacDonald, Heather, "Hispanic Family Values?" in *City Journal*, autumn 2006.

Mack Dana, *The Assault on Parenthood*, San Francisco: Encounter Books, 1997.

Macko, Lia and Kerry Rubin. *Midlife Crisis at 30.* New York: Rodale, 2004.

Magid, Ken, *High Risk Children*, New York: Bantam Books, 1987.

Marneffe de, Daphne. *Maternal Desire.* New York: Little, Brown and Company, 2004.

Marquadt, Elizabeth. *Between Two Worlds*, New York: Crown Publishers, 2005.

Maria Martinelli, in *The Day Care Decision*, by William and Wendy Dreskin. New York: 106.

McCartney, Kathleen & Deborah Phillips, Eds. *Blackwell Handbook of Early Childhood Development.* Malden, MA. Blackwell Publishing, 2006.

Mason, Mary Ann and Eve Mason Ekman, *Mothers On the Fast Track*, New York: Oxford University Press, 2007

Mogel, Wendy. *The Blessing of a Skinned Knee*, New York: Scribner, 2001.

Montagu, Ashley, "A Scientist Looks at Love." *Phi Beta Kappan*, 51, (1970).

O'Beirne Kate, *Women Who Make the World Worse.* New York: Sentinel, 2006.

OECD 2001, http://www.oecd.org/dataoecd/44/16/1942365.pdf

Office on Women's Health, Department of Health and Human Services, Breastfeeding—HHS Blueprint for Action on Breastfeeding, Washington, D.C. 2000.

Orenstein, Peggy. *Flux*, New York: Anchor Books, 2000.

Overturf Johnson, Julia. *Who's Minding the Kids? Child Care Arrangements: Winter 2002. Current Population Reports*, 70-101. U.S. Census Bureau. Washington, DC, October 2005.

Page, Clarence. Out- of-Wedlock Births in Black America, *NPR Interview*, September 27, 2005.

Peskowitz, Miriam. *The Truth Behind the Mommy Wars*. Emeryville, CA: Seal Press, 2005.

Peters, Joan K. *Not Your Mother's Life*. Cambridge, Mass.: Perseus Books, 2001.

Pryor Gale. *Nursing Mother, Working Mother: the essential guide for breastfeeding and staying close to your baby after you return to work.* http://pregnancyandbaby.com/pregnancy/baby/breastfeeding-and-bonding–Building-a-relationship-471.htm

Pryor, Karen and Gale Pryor, *Nursing Your Baby*. 4th edition. New York: Harper Resource, 2005.

Sachs, Wendy. *How She Really Does It*. Cambridge, MA: De Capo Press, 2005.

Scarr, Sandra, *Mother Care/Other Care*, (New York: Penguin Books, 1987.

Sears, William, M.D. and Martha Sears, R.N. *The Attachment Parenting Book*. New York: Little, Brown and Company, 2001.

Schore, A.N. 2002, "The Neurobiology of Attachment and early personality organization." *Journal of Prenatal and Perinatal Psychology and Health*, 16(3):249-63.

Shenk, David. *The Genius in All of Us*. New York: Doubleday, 2010.

Steiner, Leslie Morgan, *Mommy Wars*. New York: Random House, 2006.

Stobbe, Mike. "37 Percent of U.S. Births Out of Wedlock", *Associated Press*, November 21, 2006.

Stoddard Alexandra, *Mothers*. New York: William Morrow and Company, 1996.

Swedish Information Service, email – www.sweden.se

Stone Pamela, *Opting Out?* Berkeley: University of California Press, 2007.

Britto, Pia Rebello, Jeanne Brooks-Gunn, and Terri M.Griffin, "Maternal reading and teaching patterns: Associations with School readiness in low-income African American families" in *RRQ*, Vol 41, 1, Jan/Feb/Mar 2006: 68 – 86.

Tom Tugend, January 13, 2010, *Dowd's Evening in L.A. With the Rabbi*, http://www.jewishjournal.com/community/article/dowds_evening_in_la_with_the_rabbi_20100113/

Thurer, Shari L. *The Myths of Motherhood*. New York: Penguin Books, 1994.

Turnbull, Collin, *The Mountain People* (New York: Touchstone, 1987.

James M. Pethokoukis, "The Economy May Face a Shortage of Qualified Workers," *U.S .News & World Report* (June 12, 2006).

Wu, Lawrence L. and Barbara Wolfe, eds. *Out of Wedlock.* New York: Russell Sage Foundation, 2001.

Vermeer, H.J., and M.H. van Ijzendoorn. "Children's elevated cortisol levels at daycare: A review and meta-analysis." *Early Childhood Research Quarterly 21:390-40,* 2006.

Walsh, Anthony, *The Science of Love.* Buffalo, New York: Prometheus Books, 1966.

Warren, Rick, *The Purpose Driven Life,* Grand Rapid, MI: Zondervan, 2007.

Warner, Judith. *Perfect Madness.* New York: Riverhead Books, 2005.

Acknowledgements

I met John Bowlby, the father of attachment theory, many years ago in a library at Stanford University. I was writing a paper on separation anxiety of preschool children and came across Bowlby's theory of attachment. I have been impressed by his foresight. And I owe my first debt of gratitude to John Bowlby. The *Drama of the Mother-Child Bond* would have never been written without his lasting inspiration.

I owe a deep debt of gratitude to many other thinkers who encouraged the writing of this book. Especially the late Stanley I. Greenspan, of George Washington University Medical School, who was a source of inspiration with his unshakable courage to stand against the politically correct machine and underscore the importance of mother/child relationship in the early years of life, and the need to protect it.

Sharon L. Ramey, of Georgetown University Center on Health and Education, was another pillar of strength with her bold commentary on the results of the NICHD Study of Early Child Care and Youth Development (2005); and her passionate call to break the "Conspiracy of Silence" about the negative effect of daycare on young children's development.

Many other scholars and lay people contributed to the ideas expressed in this book; too many to mention in this acknowledgement. They are all given full credit in the text.

I would also like to thank my readers and friends, especially Mary Read, Dr. Marianna Kaufman, Dr. Henry and Madelyn Eisenberg, Cindi Reis, Jessica Nierad, Rabbi Charles Sherman, and Congresswoman Ann Marie Buerkle, for reading parts or the entire manuscript, and offering insightful comments; and most importantly, expressing their heartfelt excitement about this book.

To my son, Dr. Ran Anbar, many thanks for your help and encouragement throughout the long process of writing this book.

Last but not least, I owe the greatest debt of gratitude to my husband, Dr. Michael Anbar, who stood by my side throughout the lengthy process of this book's creation, patiently reading the different drafts of the manuscript, and coming to the rescue whenever computer problems showed up. I appreciate Michael, in particular, your heroic effort to see this book in print; and, the many dinners out, when working days were too long.

About The Author

ADA ANBAR holds a Ph.D. in Early Childhood Education from the University at Buffalo, and, after a 40-year teaching career, is now a full-time writer. The author of several parenting books, she lives with her husband in Fayettville, New York and Fountain Hills, Arizona, near their two sons and six grandchildren.

CPSIA information can be obtained at www.ICGtesting.com
Printed in the USA
LVOW06s0243150813

347912LV00001BA/100/P